180 Days of MATH for Prekindergarten

Darcy Mellinger, M.A.T., NBCT

Consultant

Brenda A. Van Dixhorn, M.A.Ed.
Early Elementary Educator, Minnesota

Publishing Credits

Corinne Burton, M.A.Ed., *Publisher*
Aubrie Nielsen, M.S.Ed., *EVP of Content Development*
Emily R. Smith, M.A.Ed., *VP of Content Development*
Véronique Bos, *Creative Director*
Andrew Greene, M.A.Ed., *Senior Content Manager*
Lynette Ordoñez, *Content Specialist*
Dani Neiley, *Associate Editor*
Jill Malcolm, *Multimedia Specialist*

Standards

© 2014 Mid-continent Research for Education and Learning
© Copyright 2007–2021 Texas Education Agency (TEA). All Rights Reserved.
© 2012 Mathematics Content Standards for California Public Schools by the California Department of Education
© Copyright 2010 National Governors Association Center for Best Practices and Council of Chief State School Officers. All rights reserved.
© 2021 TESOL International Association
© 2021 Board of Regents of the University of Wisconsin System

Image Credits: all images from iStock and/or Shutterstock

The classroom teacher may reproduce copies of materials in this book for classroom use only. The reproduction of any part for an entire school or school system is strictly prohibited. No part of this publication may be transmitted, stored, or recorded in any form without written permission from the publisher.

Website addresses included in this book are public domain and may be subject to changes or alterations of content after publication of this product. Shell Education does not take responsibility for the future accuracy or relevance and appropriateness of website addresses included in this book. Please contact the company if you come across any inappropriate or inaccurate website addresses, and they will be corrected in product reprints.

All companies, websites, and products mentioned in this book are registered trademarks of their respective owners or developers and are used in this book strictly for editorial purposes. No commercial claim to their use is made by the authors or the publisher.

A division of Teacher Created Materials
5482 Argosy Avenue
Huntington Beach, CA 92649-1039
www.tcmpub.com/shell-education
ISBN 978-1-0876-5203-0
© 2022 Shell Educational Publishing, Inc.

Printed by: 584728
Printed In: India
PO#: 15820

Table of Contents

Introduction 4
   What Do the Experts Say? 4
   How to Use This Book 7
   Activities Overview 10
   Standards Correlation 13

Introduction to Numbers 0–10 15
   Numbers 0–5 16
   Numbers 6–10 53

Measurement & Data 88
   Attributes 89
   Comparing Attributes 95
   Classify & Count 100

Introduction to Numbers 11–20 105
   Numbers 11–15 106
   Numbers 16–20 141

Geometry 176
   Introducing Shapes 177
   Above & Below 182
   Beside & Next To 185
   Behind & In Front 188
   Compare, Create & Compose Shapes 191

Review 0–20, Measurement & Shapes 194

Answer Key 199

Appendixes 206
   References Cited 206
   Digital Resources 207

Introduction

What Do the Experts Say?

Welcome to *180 Days of Math for Prekindergarten*! The most important concepts students will learn prior to entering kindergarten are practiced in the pages of this book. These practice pages can also be useful for students in kindergarten and first grade or older students who need extra support in learning the foundational skills of mathematics.

Foundations

In this book, students practice foundational math concepts. Learning these introductory ideas about mathematics is essential for young students. According to Robert Marzano, "practice has always been, and always will be, a necessary ingredient to learning procedural knowledge at a level at which students execute it independently" (2010, 83). Practicing these core skills may be key to students' success in mathematics. Research reported in the American Psychological Association article "School Readiness and Later Achievement" supports early academic focus on math skills to have long-term impacts on students:

> First, math and reading skills at the point of school entry are consistently associated with higher levels of academic performance in later grades. Particularly impressive is the predictive power of early math skills, which supports the wisdom of experimental evaluations of promising early math intervention. (Duncan et al. 2007)

Another important aspect of teaching young learners is supporting a positive outlook of math and helping students see themselves with a growth mindset. In *Growing Mathematical Minds: Conversations Between Developmental Psychologists and Early Childhood Teacher*s (2019), McCray et al. discuss the need for developing foundational math knowledge along with fostering students to develop positive attitudes toward math. Students are best able to think mathematically when they have positive feelings about the subject matter. We have the privilege to encourage the joy of learning math through this book.

Introduction

Repetition

Repetition is a key to success for learners. It is estimated that 85–90 percent of brain growth occurs in the first five years of life (First Things First 2017). Introducing children to the foundational skills of mathematics during those first five years of life sets them up for greater achievement in elementary school.

Practice, Assess, and Diagnose

The practice pages in this book provide instructional opportunities for each day of the school year. Activities are organized into content themes. The mathematics skills learned each day are aligned to standards. In *180 Days of Math for Prekindergarten,* the best practices of instruction have been considered to create a sequential book to support students as they learn math skills. Use the daily activities to assess student growth as they develop mathematical skills. The wide variety of activities offered on each page creates several opportunities to diagnose student needs for additional support or repetition. Students will be engaged and challenged each day in this mathematical journey!

Introduction

What Do the Experts Say? (cont.)

Sequence of Learning

The order in which students learn basic math skills is important. It is similar to the construction of a building, where the foundation is secured as the first step. The order of these skills was given great consideration during the creation of this resource. Make sure to follow the pages in the order they appear to gain the most from its contents.

Emphasis has been given to counting and cardinality, operations and algebraic thinking, and numbers and operations in base-ten skills. Students are first introduced to numbers 0 through 5, followed by 6 through 10. In each section, students learn to name the number, count by ones up to the given number, tell how many are in a collection of objects, identify the number compared to other numbers, write the number correctly, and count on from the given number. They learn to add, subtract, compose, and decompose numbers up to 10. They also practice comparing numbers to see if one is greater than, less than, or equal to another.

1 2 3 4 5 6 7 8 9 10

Students continue their learning with measurement and data. They are introduced to the concepts of length, weight, and height. Classifying objects is also explored before learners dive back into practicing counting and cardinality. Students use numbers 11 through 15 followed by 16 through 20 to practice the same skills learned with numbers 0 through 10.

In the geometry section, learners are introduced to squares, circles, triangles, rectangles, and hexagons. They also determine the positions of shapes as they compare to the positions of other shapes.

The last five days in this book are a final review in which students combine the skills previously learned so they can successfully start practicing their mathematical skills. Finally, there are extra files to support students' learning in the Digital Resources as they conclude their day-by-day journey to learn about math.

How to Use This Book

Introducing the Concept Pages

To help teachers and caregivers understand each new section in *180 Days of Math for Prekindergarten*, there are Introducing the Concept pages to begin the sections. These pages support adults as they guide young learners through each topic.

Section overviews explain new concepts covered in the upcoming pages.

Materials lists provide suggestions that will help students as they complete the activities.

Additional recommendations are provided to help teachers and caregivers support student learning.

Introducing the Concept

Numbers 0–10

Learning All About 0–10

In this section, students are introduced to numbers 0 through 10. They practice the names of the numbers, how to count up to 10, and how to identify numbers 0 to 10 when they are mixed in with other numbers. Students learn the correct way to make each number from 0 through 10. Next, they explore adding and subtracting with numbers up to 10. Students also learn to compose and decompose using these numbers. This section of learning ends with students comparing numbers to see if a number is greater than, less than, or equal to another number.

What You May Need

- jumbo pencils or short golf pencils
- crayons, colored pencils, etc.
- modeling clay, interlocking cubes, coins

Understanding the Activities

As you work through these pages, here are some ways to further support student learning:

- Discuss the names of the numbers as they are introduced.
- Read directions to students. Follow the directions one step at a time, allowing enough time for students to complete each task before moving to the next step in the directions.
- As students write, double-check that they are writing numbers accurately by following the numbers and arrows. The repetition when learning to write numbers helps them later with math fluency.
- If students need extra support with their fine-motor skills, you may want to write the numbers with highlighters or light markers so students can trace over them more easily.

Introduction

How to Use This Book (cont.)

Using the Practice Pages

The practice pages in this book provide instructional opportunities for 180 days. Activities are organized into content themes. Each day's math skills are aligned to mathematics standards that can be found on pages 13–14.

Students practice counting objects and writing numbers to build fluency and recognition.

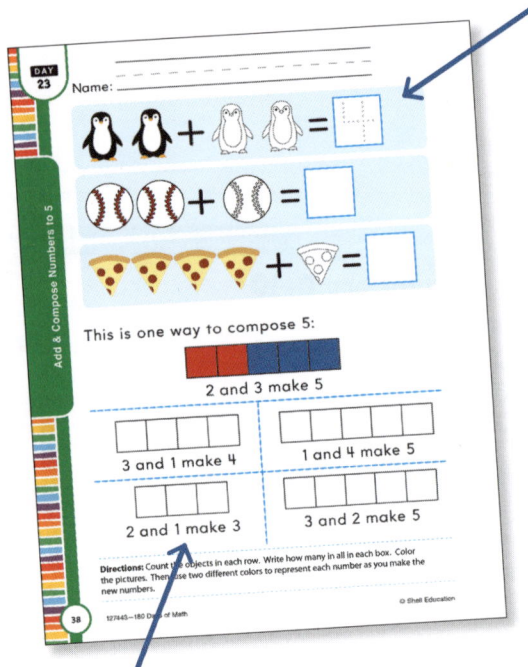

Students get multiple opportunities to make numbers in a variety of ways.

Easy-to-follow directions help adults support students as they complete activities.

Using the "Sky, Fence, and Grass" to Write

There are different ways to write numbers. This book suggests forming numbers using methods that generally do not require students to lift their pencils off the page. To support students in writing numbers, this book has writing lines with "sky, fence, and grass." This is a concept reviewed throughout the 180 days.

Use the sky, fence, and grass to help students understand how to use the writing lines: sky = top line, fence = midline, and grass = bottom line.

Introduction

Proper Pencil Grip

It is important for children to learn how to properly grip their pencils early. Each student will naturally find their dominant hand. If a student writes with both their right and their left hand, brain research indicates that it is preferred to allow them to write with both hands. Younger students may have to grow into this grip, so encourage students to try this grip when you see that they are ready. The best pencil grip for children is with their pointer finger on the top, thumb on the side, and three fingers below the pencil to support the grip. The grip of the pencil is about one inch from the tip of the pencil. When students write throughout the pages of this book, encourage proper pencil grip.

Teach students to use sharpened pencils when it is time to do math. Students will use their nondominant hands to hold down their papers or books. Posture is important, so invite students to sit tall with their backs supported by chairs. Their chairs should be a comfortable distance from the tables where they are working. Teach students to press down on their pencils with medium strength—not too hard and not too softly. Flexible seating is encouraged after proper grip and writing of numbers has been mastered. To learn more about this topic, you can check out *How to Hold a Pencil* by Megan Hirsch.

Introduction

Activities Overview

Over the upcoming 180 days of learning, expect students to grow in their enthusiasm for mathematics. Learners will emerge as courageous mathematicians as they observe how these math concepts relate to their everyday lives.

Numbers 0–20

Students learn counting and cardinality, operations and algebraic thinking, and numbers and operations in base-ten skills with numbers from 0 through 20. Activities with these numbers are introduced gradually in sets: 0 to 5, 6 to 10, 11 to 15, and finally 16 to 20. Students complete the following activities with these numbers:

Name Numbers 0–20	Students learn the name of each number 0–20 and count up to that number.
Count by Ones to 20	Students practice counting up to 20 and determine least and most to compare amounts.
Identify Numbers 0–20	Students practice finding a given number from 0 to 20 among other numbers. Students find the number written on everyday objects. They count to tell how many of a given number.
Write Numbers from 0–20	Students learn how to write each number on writing lines using the "sky, fence, and grass." Students also count on from a given number.
Add & Compose Numbers to 20	Students practice addition word problems by "putting together" objects. They practice using 5-frames and 10-frames to compose numbers.
Subtract & Decompose Numbers to 20	Students practice subtraction word problems by "taking away" objects. They practice using 5-frames and 10-frames to decompose numbers.
Compare Numbers Up to 20	Students compare two numbers to see if one is greater than, less than, or equal to another.

Introduction

Measurement & Data

In the Measurement & Data pages, students learn the attributes of length, weight, and height. Students compare attributes of shapes. They also determine if there are more or less of one shape compared to the quantity of others. Finally, they practice classifying and counting objects in a category.

Geometry

In this section, students are introduced to geometric shapes. They practice with squares, circles, triangles, rectangles, and hexagons. They compare the locations of objects using the words *above* or *below*, *beside* or *next to*, and *behind* or *in front of* other shapes. Finally, students practice creating and composing geometric shapes.

Introduction

Activities Overview (cont.)

Review Pages

Throughout this resource, students have opportunities to continuously review counting and cardinality, operations and algebraic thinking, and numbers and operations in base-ten skills. Regular review is emphasized in *180 Days of Math for Prekindergarten* to support student retention of these key skills. At the end of the book, students use these key skills along with measurement, data, and geometry. Embark upon this journey of discovery with students to create positive attitudes about mathematics in prekindergarten. On the last day of practice (Day 180), you may use the certificate to celebrate students' learning achievements.

Standards Correlations

Shell Education is committed to producing educational materials that are research and standards based. To support this effort, this resource is correlated to the academic standards of all 50 states, the District of Columbia, the Department of Defense Dependent Schools, and the Canadian provinces. A correlation is also provided for key professional educational organizations.

To print a customized correlation report for your state, visit our website at www.tcmpub.com/administrators/correlations and follow the online directions. If you require assistance in printing correlation reports, please contact the Customer Service Department at 1-800-858-7339.

College and Career Readiness Standards

Counting and Cardinality	**Know number names and the count sequence.** • Count to 100 by ones. • Count forward beginning from a given number within the known sequence. • Write numbers from 0 to 20. Represent a number of objects with a written numeral 0–20. **Count to tell the number of objects.** • Understand the relationship between numbers and quantities; connect counting to cardinality. • When counting objects, say the number names in the standard order, pairing each object with one and only one number name and each number name with one and only one object. • Understand that the last number name said tells the number of objects counted. The number of objects is the same regardless of their arrangement or the order in which they were counted. • Understand that each successive number name refers to a quantity that is one larger. • Count to answer "how many?" questions about as many as 20 things arranged in a line, a rectangular array, a circle, or as many as 10 things in a scattered configuration; given a number from 1–20, count out that many objects.
Numbers and Operations in Base Ten	**Work with numbers 11–19 to gain foundations for place value.** • Compose and decompose numbers from 11 to 19 into ten ones and some further ones, e.g., by using objects or drawings, and record each composition or decomposition by a drawing or equation (e.g., 18 = 10 + 8); understand that these numbers are composed of ten ones and zero, one, two, three, four, five, six, seven, eight, or nine ones.

Introduction

Standards Correlations (cont.)

Operations and Algebraic Thinking	**Understand addition as putting together and adding to, and understand subtraction as taking apart and taking from.** • Represent addition and subtraction with objects, fingers, mental images, drawings, sounds (e.g., claps), acting out situations, verbal explanations, expressions, or equations. • Solve addition and subtraction word problems, and add and subtract within 10, e.g., by using objects or drawings to represent the problem. • Decompose numbers less than or equal to 10 into pairs in more than one way, e.g., by using objects or drawings, and record each decomposition by a drawing or equation (e.g., $5 = 2 + 3$ and $5 = 4 + 1$). • For any number from 1 to 9, find the number that makes 10 when added to the given number, e.g., by using objects or drawings, and record the answer with a drawing or equation. • Fluently add and subtract within 5.
Measurement and Data	**Describe and compare measurable attributes.** • Describe measurable attributes of objects, such as length or weight. Describe several measurable attributes of a single object. • Directly compare two objects with a measurable attribute in common to see which object has "more of"/"less of" the attribute, and describe the difference. *For example, directly compare the heights of two children and describe one child as taller/shorter.*
Geometry	**Identify and describe shapes (squares, circles, triangles, rectangles, hexagons).** • Describe objects in the environment using names of shapes, and describe the relative positions of these objects using terms such as *above, below, beside, in front of, behind,* or *next to.* • Correctly name shapes regardless of their orientations or overall size. **Analyze, compare, create, and compose shapes.** • Analyze and compare two-dimensional shapes in different sizes and orientations.

TESOL and WIDA Standards

In this book, the following English language development standard is met: Standard 1: English language learners communicate for social and instructional purposes within the school setting.

Introducing the Concept

Introduction to Numbers 0–10

Learning All About 0–10

In this section, students are introduced to numbers 0 through 10. They practice the names of the numbers, how to count up to 10, and how to identify numbers 0 to 10 when they are mixed in with other numbers. Students learn how to write each number from 0 through 10. Next, they explore adding and subtracting with numbers up to 10. Students also learn to compose and decompose these numbers. This section of learning ends with students comparing numbers to see if a number is greater than, less than, or equal to another number.

What You May Need

- jumbo pencils or short golf pencils
- crayons, colored pencils, etc.
- small, nonchoking objects for covering-number activities (modeling clay, interlocking cubes, beans, coins, etc.)

Understanding the Activities

As you work through these pages, here are some ways to further support student learning:

- Discuss the names of the numbers as they are introduced.
- Read directions to students. Follow the directions one step at a time, allowing enough time for students to complete each task before moving to the next step in the directions.
- As students write, double-check that they are writing numbers accurately by following the numbers and arrows. The repetition when learning to write numbers helps them later with math fluency.
- If students need extra support with their fine-motor skills, you may want to write the numbers with highlighters or light markers so students can trace over them.
- Discuss the symbols > (greater than), < (less than), and = with students when completing the comparing numbers section. Read the number sentences aloud with students to reinforce what the symbols mean.

DAY 1

Name: _____

Name Numbers 0–5

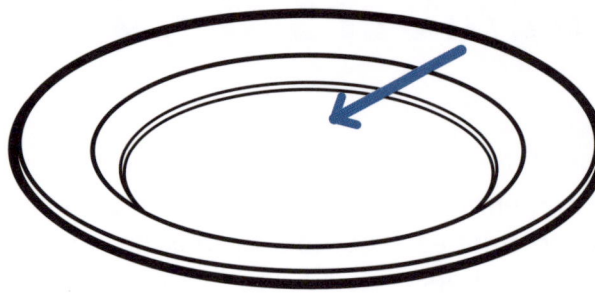
0 cookies

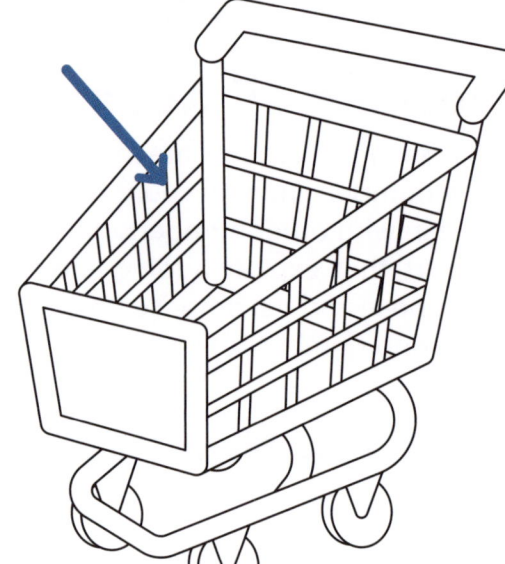
0 items

zero

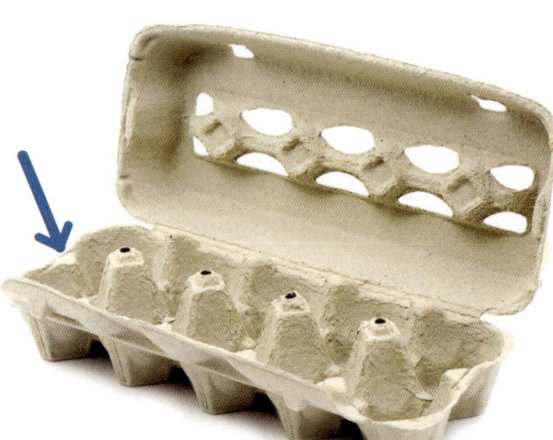
0 eggs

Time to Draw

Directions: Trace the 0 at least 10 times with your finger. Say its name as you do this. Count the objects in each picture. Color the pictures. Circle each number 0. Then, draw yourself with 0 objects in your hands.

Name: _____

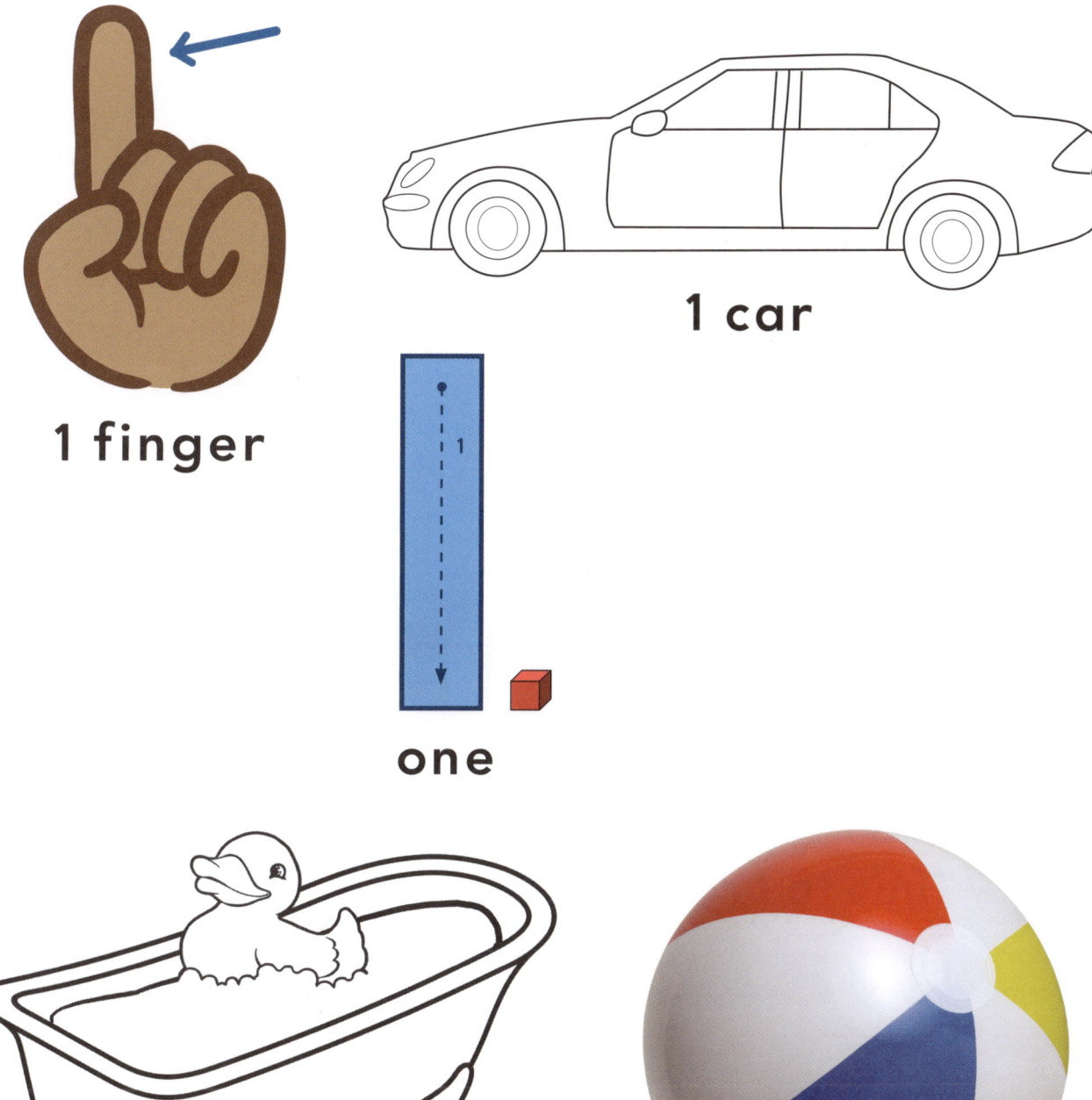

1 finger

1 car

one

1 duck

1 ball

Directions: Trace the 1 at least 10 times with your finger. Say its name as you do this. Count the objects in each picture. Color the pictures. Circle each number 1. Then, make the number 1 with your body.

DAY 3

Name Numbers 0–5

Name: _____

2 wings

2 wheels

two

2 socks

Time to Draw

Directions: Trace the 2 at least 10 times with your finger. Say its name as you do this. Count the objects in each picture. Color the pictures. Circle each number 2. Then, go on a scavenger hunt to look for objects that come in twos. Draw what you find.

Name: _____

DAY 4

Name Numbers 0–5

3 cupcakes

3 colors

3

three

3 pigs

Directions: Trace the 3 at least 10 times with your finger. Say its name as you do this. Count the objects in each picture. Color the pictures. Circle each number 3. Then, find and put a box around the number 3 in the images.

© Shell Education

127443—180 Days of Math

19

DAY 5

Name: _____

Name Numbers 0–5

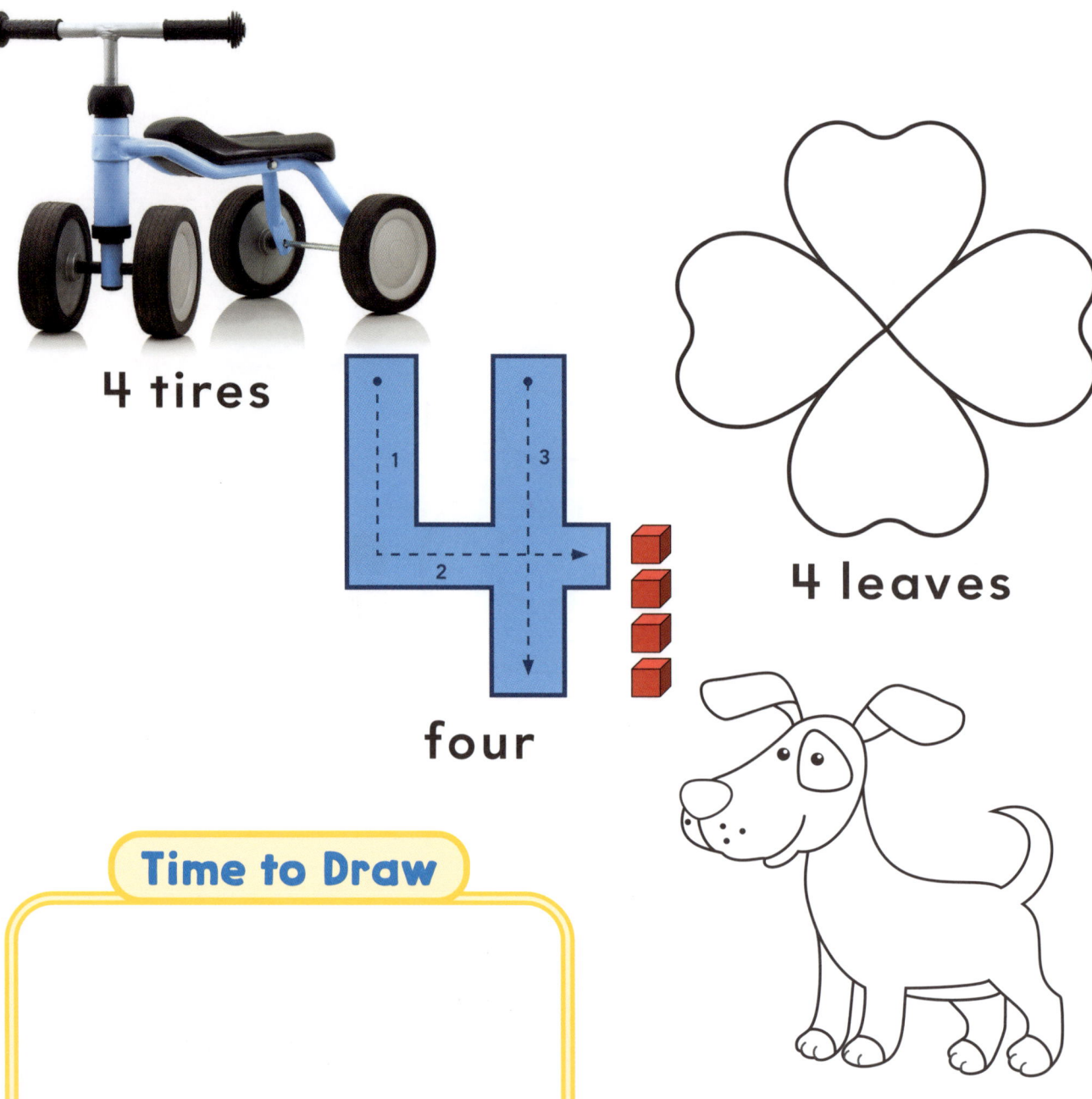

4 tires

four

4 leaves

4 legs

Time to Draw

Directions: Trace the 4 at least 10 times with your finger. Say its name as you do this. Count the objects in each picture. Color the pictures. Circle each number 4. Then, draw 4 objects.

Name: _____

DAY 6

Name Numbers 0–5

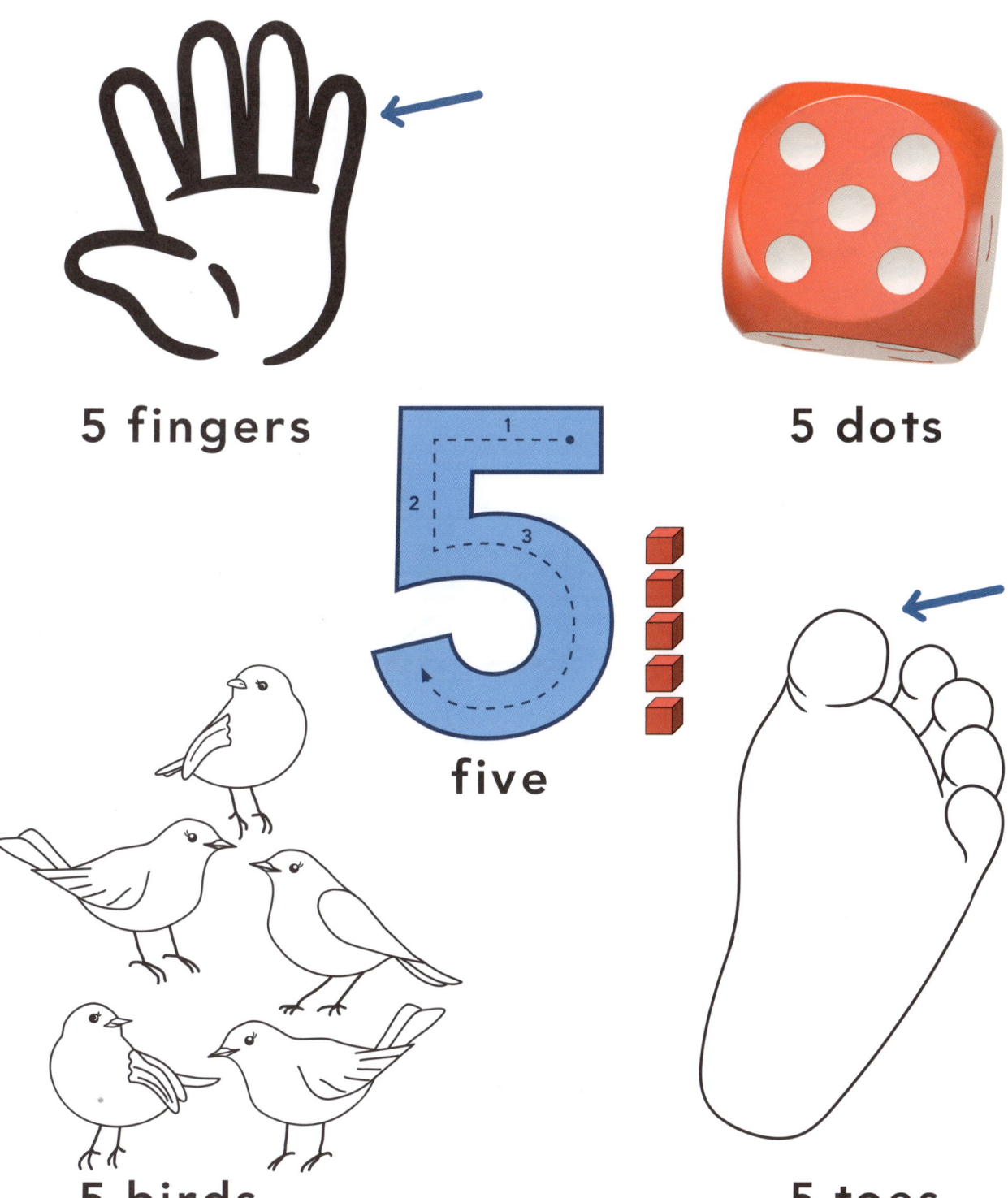

5 fingers

5 dots

five

5 birds

5 toes

Directions: Trace the 5 at least 10 times with your finger. Say its name as you do this. Count the objects in each picture. Color the pictures. Circle each number 5. Then, count 5 fingers on your hand or a partner's hand.

DAY 7

Name: _____

Count by Ones to 5

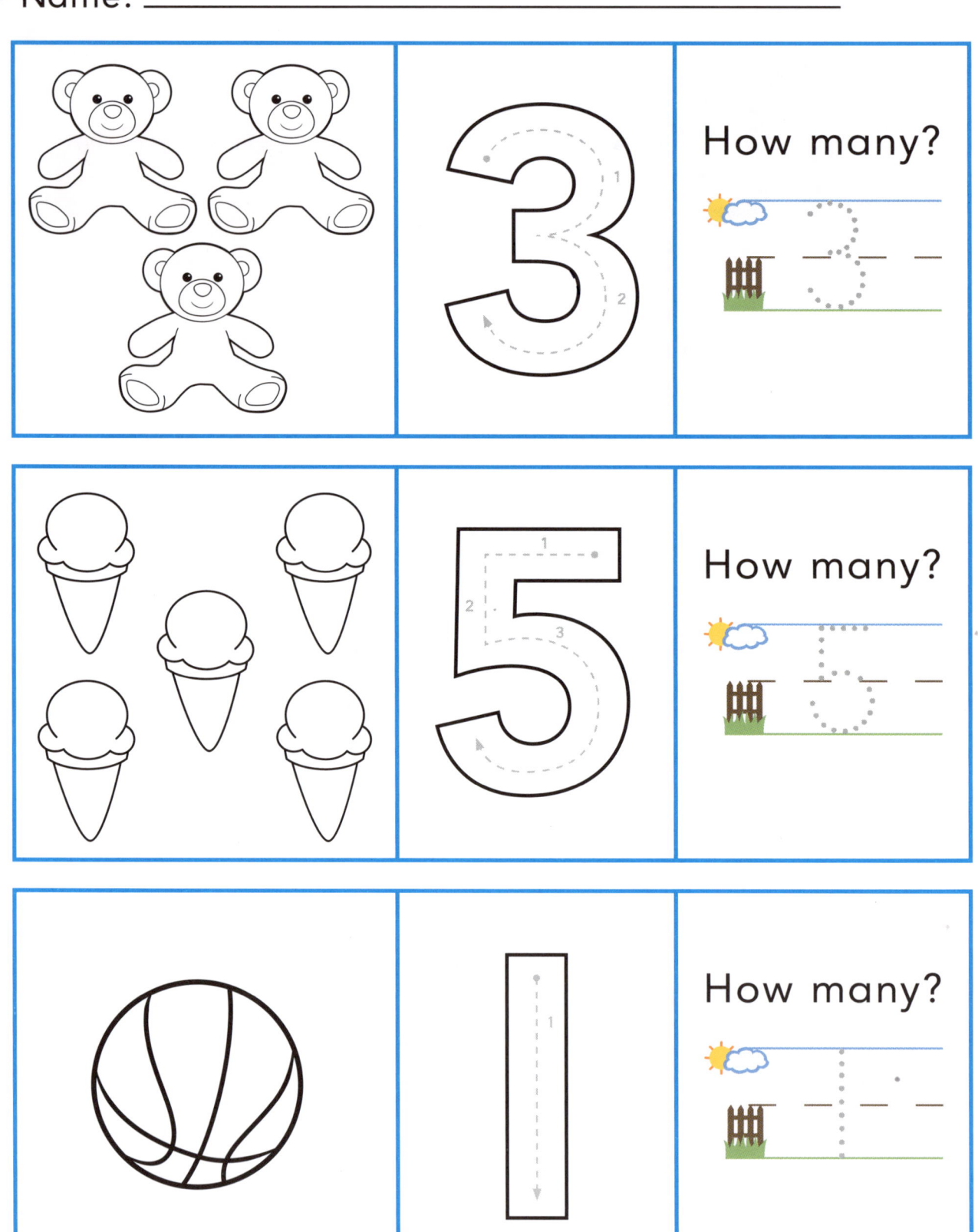

Directions: Count the objects in each row. Write the number of objects in each row. Color the pictures and numbers.

Name: _____

DAY 8

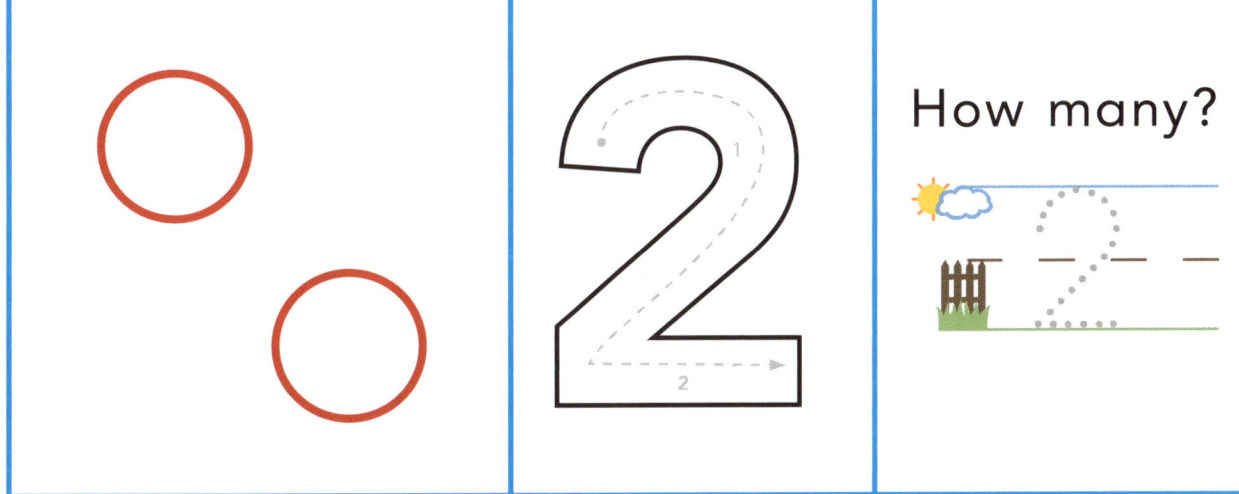

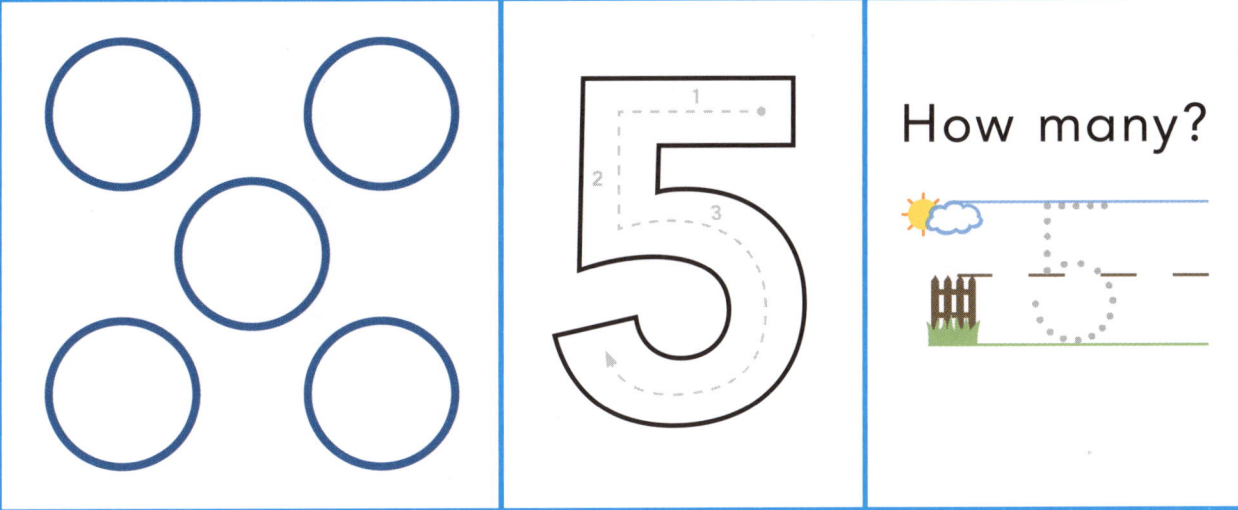

Which number is less: 2 or 5?

Directions: Place one small object in each red circle. Count the objects in the red circles. Write the number of objects on the line. Color the red circles. Do the same steps for the blue circles. Then, answer the question.

Count by Ones to 5

DAY 9

Name: _____

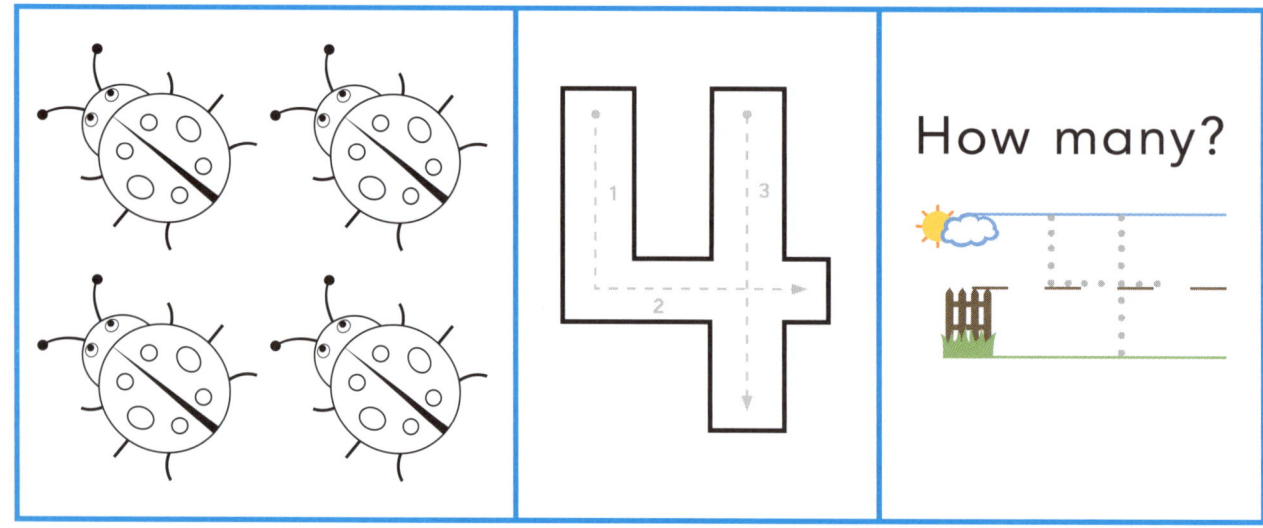

Directions: Count the objects in each row. Write the number of objects in each row. Color the pictures and numbers.

Name: _____

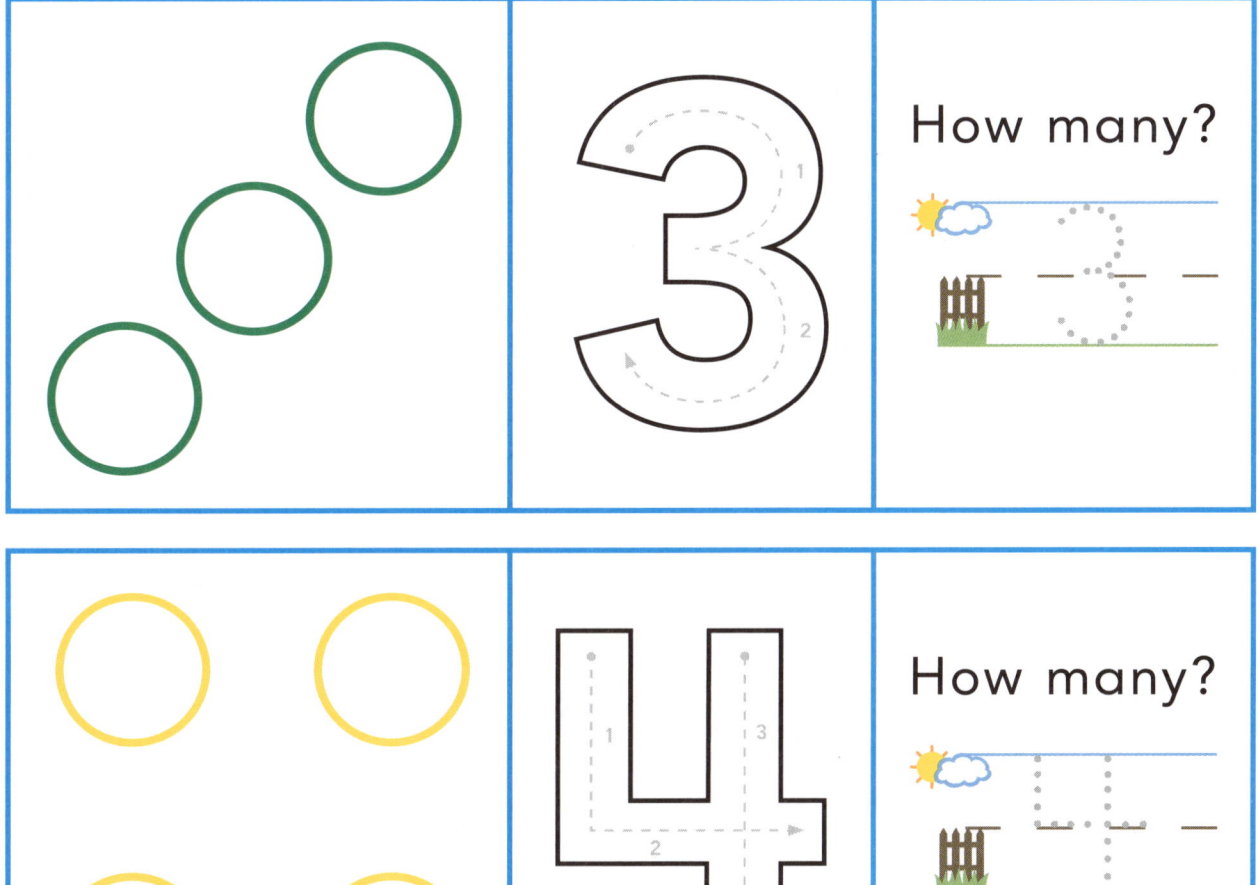

Directions: Place one small object in each green circle. Count the objects in the green circles. Write the number of objects on the line. Color the green circles. Do the same steps for the yellow circles. Then, answer the question.

Which number is more: 3 or 4?

DAY 11

Name: _____

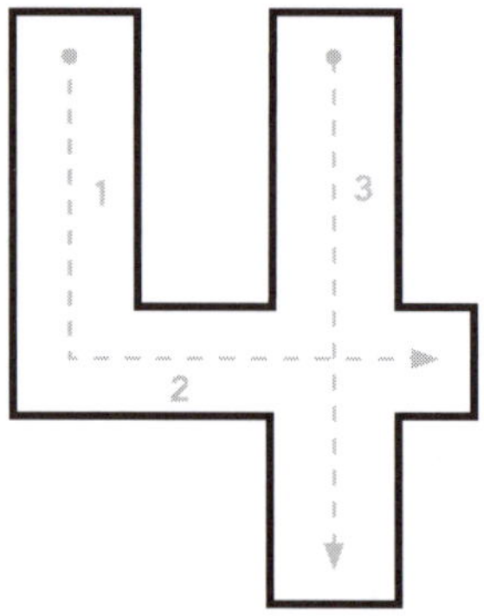

Count by Ones to 5

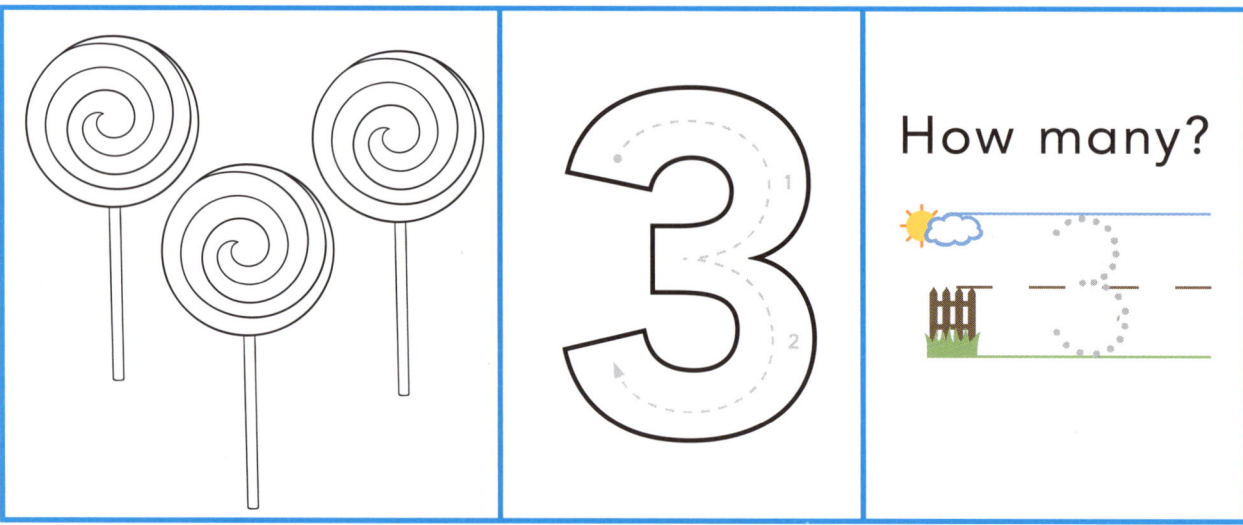

Directions: Count the objects in each row. Write the number of objects in each row. Color the pictures and numbers.

Name: _____

DAY 12

0	4	3	4	4
3	2	0	5	5
2	0	1	2	3
4	5	4	0	1
1	3	2	1	2
5	1	3	3	0

Identify Numbers 0–5

Directions: Find every number 0, and color those squares blue. Answer the question. Then, make the number 0 with small objects.

How many of the number 0 did you find?

DAY 13

Name: _____

Identify Numbers 0–5

Directions: Find and circle every number 1. Color the drawings of the number 1. Then, make the number 1 with small objects.

Name: _____

3	4	0	3	4
5	2	3	5	5
1	0	2	1	3
2	3	1	0	1
4	5	4	2	0
3	1	5	4	2

DAY 14

Identify Numbers 0–5

How many 2s did you find?

Directions: Find every number 2, and color those squares red. Answer the question. Then, make the number 2 with small objects.

DAY 15

Name: _____

Identify Numbers 0–5

Directions: Find and circle every number 3. Color the drawings of the number 3. Then, make the number 3 with your body and a partner.

Name: _____

2	4	3	3	5
1	2	1	5	3
5	0	4	0	0
3	5	2	1	2
4	3	5	4	1
0	1	0	2	4

How many 4s did you find?

Directions: Find every number 4, and color those squares green. Answer the question. Then, make the number 4 with clay or small objects.

DAY 17

Name: _____

Directions: Find and circle every number 5. Color the drawings of the number 5. Then, make the number 5 with clay or small objects.

Name: _____

DAY 18

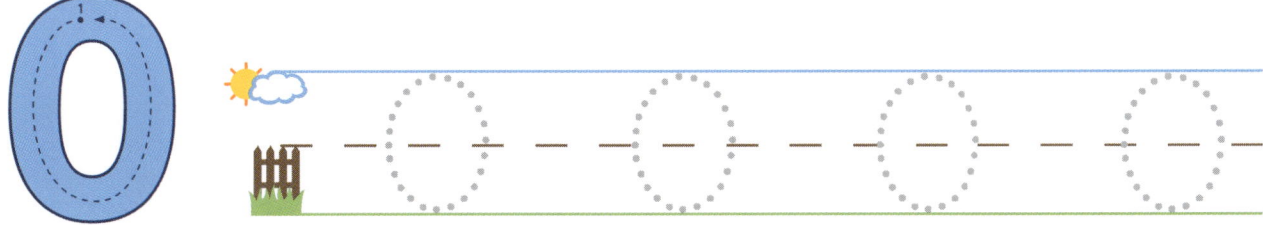

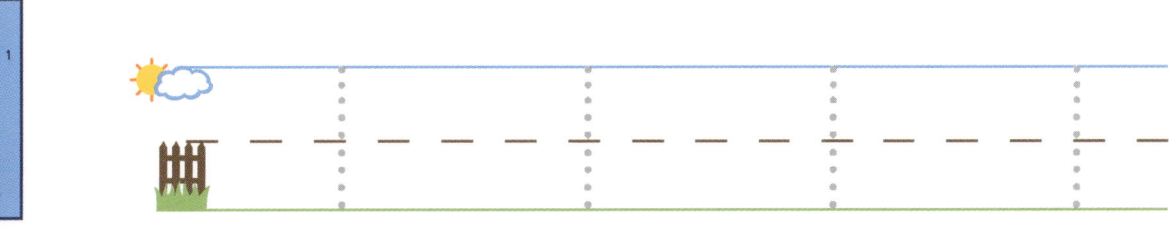

Count on...

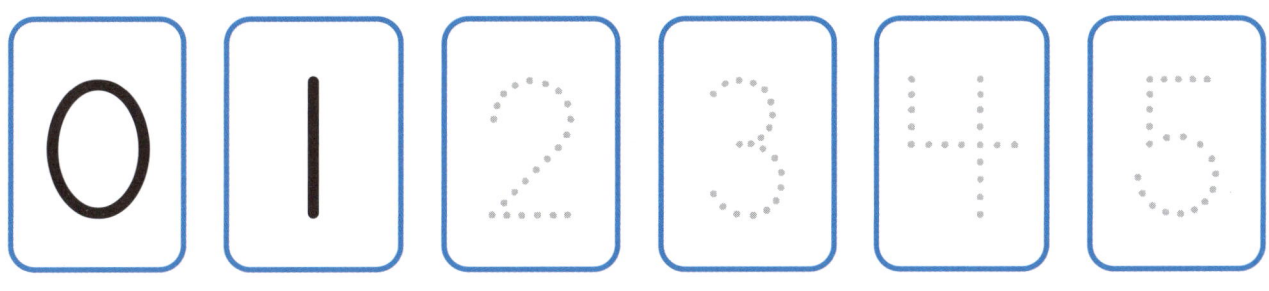

Directions: Skywrite the number 0 five times in the air with an invisible pencil. Trace the number 0, and write it on your own. Skywrite the number 1 five times in the air. Trace the number 1, and write it on your own. Count the strawberry. Then, count on from 1 to fill in the missing numbers. Say each number as you write it.

Write Numbers from 0–5

DAY 19

Name: _____

Write Numbers from 0–5

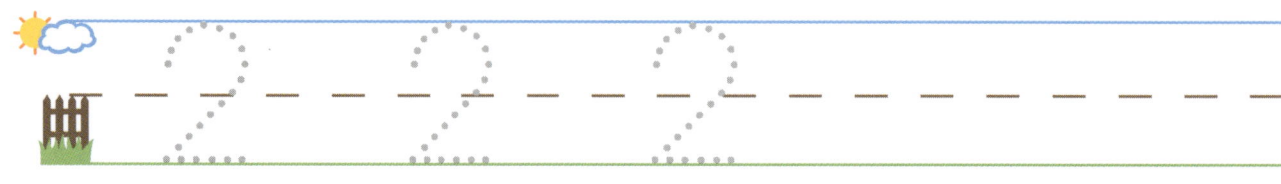
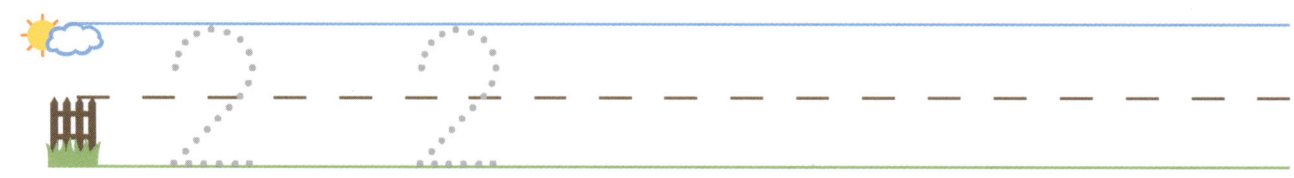

Count on...

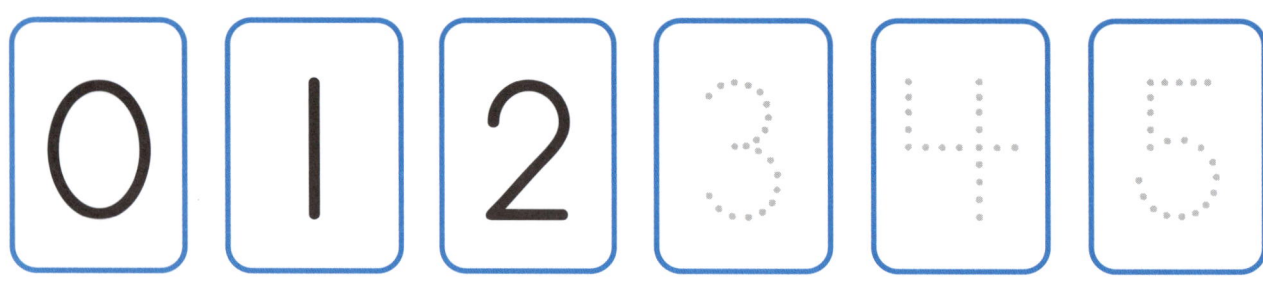

Directions: Skywrite the number 2 five times in the air with an invisible pencil. Trace the number 2, and write it on your own. Count the bears. Then, count on from 2 to fill in the missing numbers. Say each number as you write it.

Name: _____

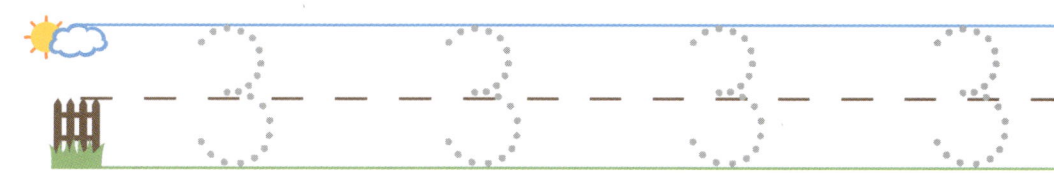
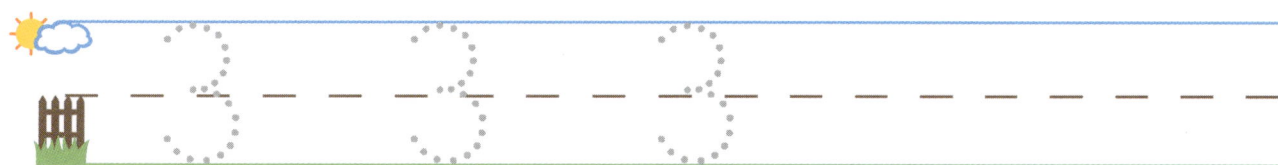

Count on...

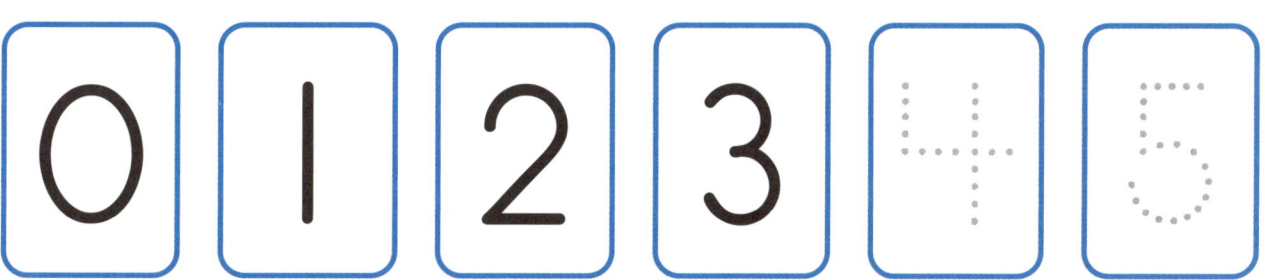

Directions: Skywrite the number 3 five times in the air with an invisible pencil. Trace the number 3, and write it on your own. Count the dogs. Then, count on from 3 to fill in the missing numbers. Say each number as you write it.

DAY 21

Name: _____

Write Numbers from 0–5

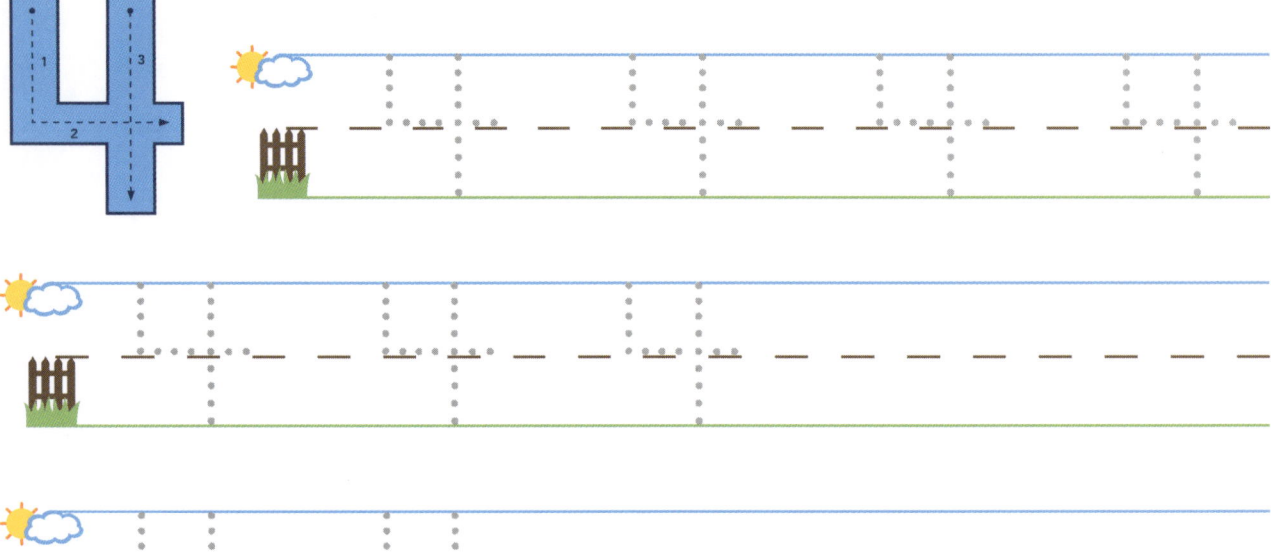

Count on...

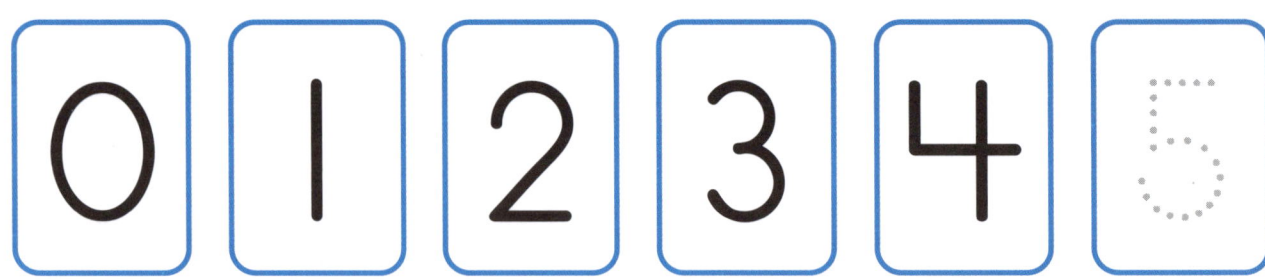

Directions: Skywrite the number 4 five times in the air with an invisible pencil. Trace the number 4, and write it on your own. Count the foxes. Then, count on from 4 to fill in the missing number. Say the number as you write it.

Name: _____

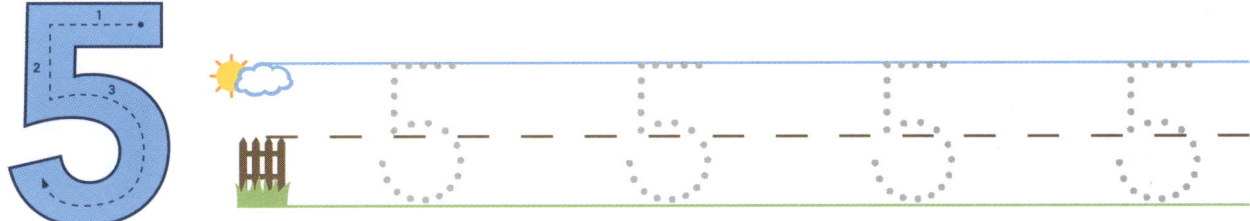

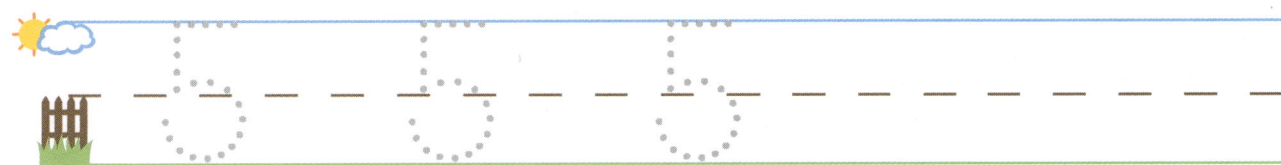

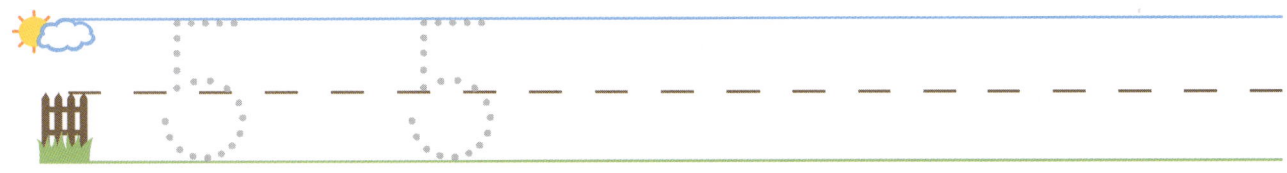

Count on...

Directions: Skywrite the number 5 five times in the air with an invisible pencil. Trace the number 5, and write it on your own. Count the umbrellas. Then, count on from 2 to fill in the missing numbers. Say each number as you write it.

DAY 22

Write Numbers from 0–5

DAY 23

Name: _____

This is one way to compose 5:

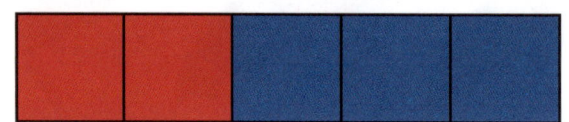

2 and 3 make 5

☐☐☐☐ 3 and 1 make 4	☐☐☐☐☐ 1 and 4 make 5
☐☐☐ 2 and 1 make 3	☐☐☐☐☐ 3 and 2 make 5

Directions: Count the objects in each row. Write how many in all in each box. Color the pictures. Then, use two different colors to represent each number as you make the new numbers.

Name: _____

DAY 24

This is one way to compose 4:

1 and 3 make 4

2 and 2 make 4	3 and 2 make 5
1 and 2 make 3	4 and 1 make 5

Add & Compose Numbers to 5

Directions: Count the objects in each row. Write how many in all in each box. Color the pictures. Then, use two different colors to represent each number as you make the new numbers.

DAY 25

Name: _____

🐞🐞🐞🐞 + 🐞 = ☐

🌼🌼 + 🌼🌼 = ☐

🍔🍔 + 🍔 = ☐

🐼 + 🐼 = ☐

This is one way to compose 3:

1 and 2 make 3

1 and 1 make 2

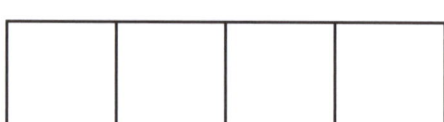

1 and 3 make 4

Directions: Count the objects in each row. Write how many in all in each box. Color the pictures. Then, use two different colors to represent each number as you make the new numbers.

Name: _____

DAY 26

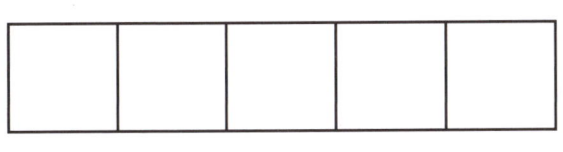

4 and 1 make 5

2 and 1 make 3

Directions: Count the objects in each row. Write how many in all in each box. Color the pictures. Then, use two different colors to represent each number as you make the new numbers.

Add & Compose Numbers to 5

DAY 27

Name: _____

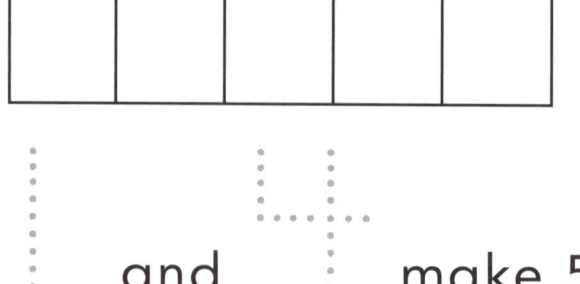

2 and 1 make 3

----

and 4 make 5

Directions: Count the objects in each row. Write how many in all in each box. Color the pictures. Trace the numbers. Then, use two different colors to represent each number as you make the new numbers.

Name: _____

5 − 3 = 2

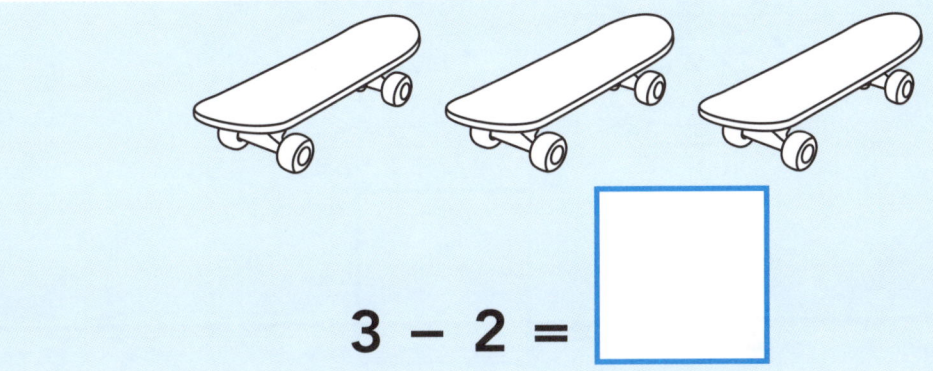

3 − 2 =

This is one way to decompose 5:

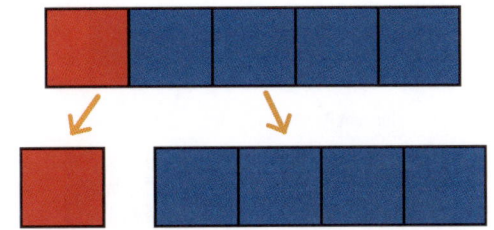

5 made with 1 and 4

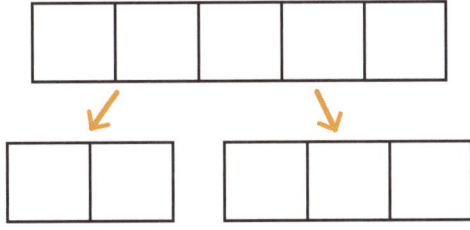

5 made with 2 and 3

Directions: Count the objects in each section. Mark an *X* on the objects taken away. Color the objects that are left over. Write the amount in each box. Then, use two different colors to show how you decomposed the number.

DAY 29

Name: _____

$3 - 3 = \boxed{}$

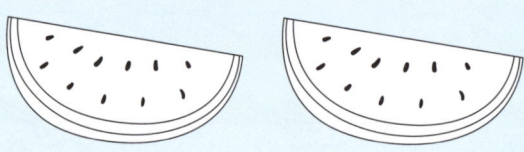

$2 - 1 = \boxed{}$

This is one way to decompose 4:

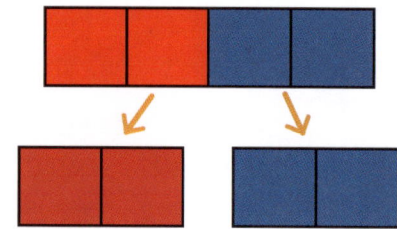

4 made with 2 and 2

- -

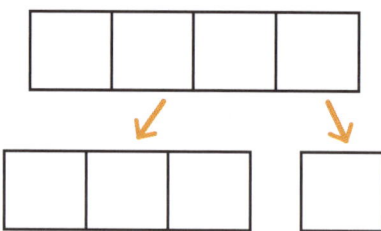

4 made with 3 and 1

Directions: Count the objects in each section. Mark an *X* on the objects taken away. Color the objects that are left over. Write the amount in each box. Then, use two different colors to show how you decomposed the number.

Name: _____

4 − 3 = ☐

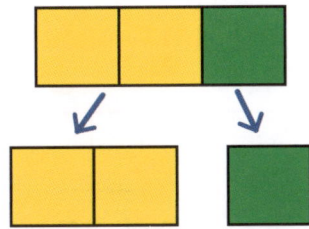

2 − 2 = ☐

This is one way to decompose 3:

[yellow, yellow, green]
↙   ↘
[yellow, yellow]   [green]

3 made with 2 and 1

- -

[☐ ☐ ☐]
↙   ↘
[☐]   [☐ ☐]

3 made with 1 and 2

Directions: Count the objects in each section. Mark an *X* on the objects taken away. Color the objects that are left over. Write the amount in each box. Then, use two different colors to show how you decomposed the number.

DAY 30

Subtract & Decompose Numbers to 5

DAY 31

Name: _____

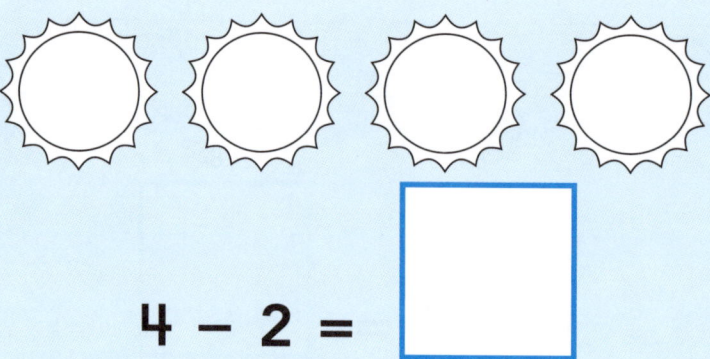

4 − 2 =

3 − 2 =

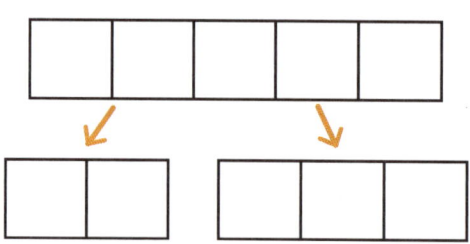

5 made with 2 and 3

- -

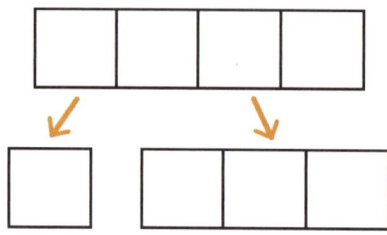

4 made with 1 and 3

Directions: Count the objects in each section. Mark an X on the objects taken away. Color the objects that are left over. Write the amount in each box. Then, use two different colors to show how you decomposed the numbers.

Name: _____

5 − 4 = ☐

4 − 1 = ☐

3 − 1 = ☐

5 − 3 = ☐

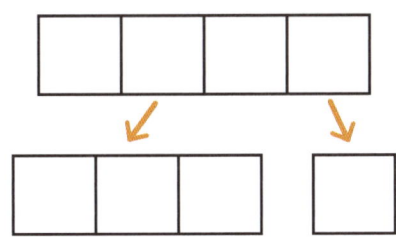

4 made with  and

Directions: Count the objects in each section. Mark an *X* on the objects taken away. Color the objects that are left over. Write the amount in each box. Then, use two different colors to show how you decomposed the number.

DAY 33

Name: _____

5  2   3 = 3   1   4

Remember that a shark ALWAYS wants to eat the bigger number!

Compare Numbers Up to 5

5 (>) = < 3

4 > = < 1

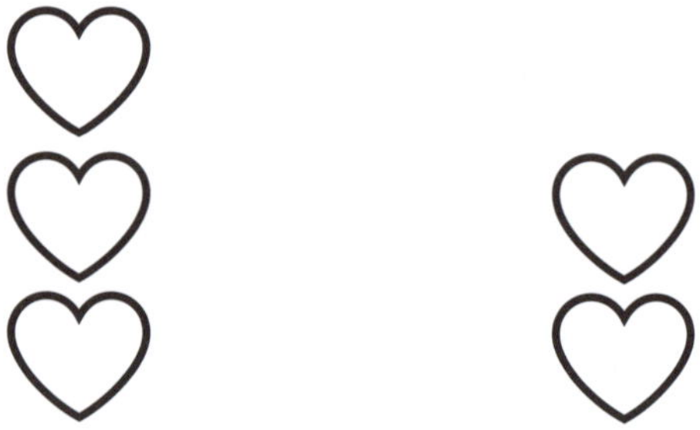

3 > = < 2

1 > = < 2

Directions: Count the objects in each section. Compare the two numbers in each section. Circle one of these signs > = <. Color the pictures. The first one has been done for you.

Name: _____

3  2   4 = 4   3  4

Remember that a shark ALWAYS wants to eat the bigger number!

DAY 34

Compare Numbers Up to 5

5 > = < 5

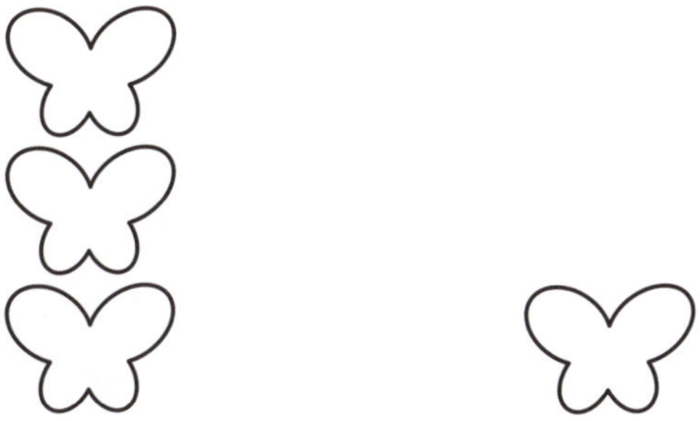

3 > = < 1

4 > = < 2

3 > = < 5

Directions: Count the objects in each section. Compare the two numbers in each section. Circle one of these signs > = <. Color the pictures.

DAY 35

Name: _____

 3 > 1   1 = 1   1 < 4

Remember that a shark ALWAYS wants to eat the bigger number!

Compare Numbers Up to 5

4   > = <   3

2   > = <   5

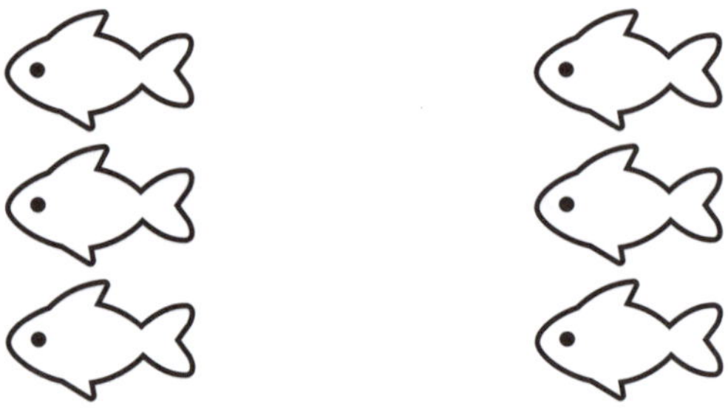

3   > = <   3

5   > = <   4

Directions: Count the objects in each section. Compare the two numbers in each section. Circle one of these signs > = <. Color the pictures.

Name: _____

DAY 36

5  1   2 = 2   1  3

Remember that a shark ALWAYS wants to eat the bigger number!

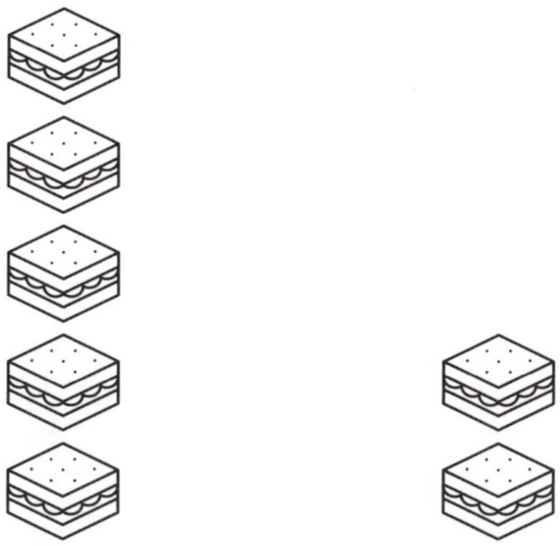

Compare Numbers Up to 5

5   > = <   2

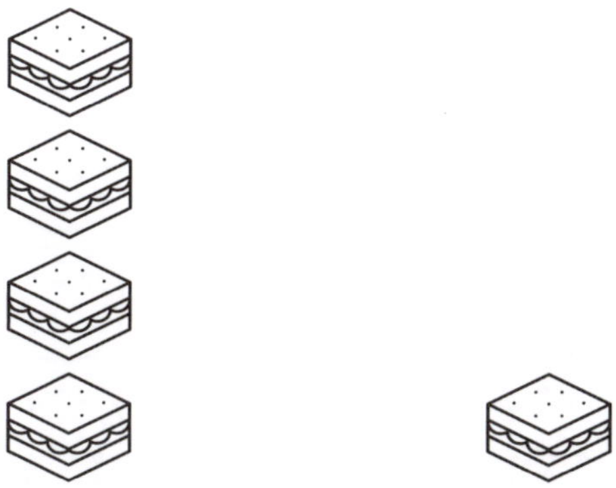

4   > = <   1

3   > = <   2

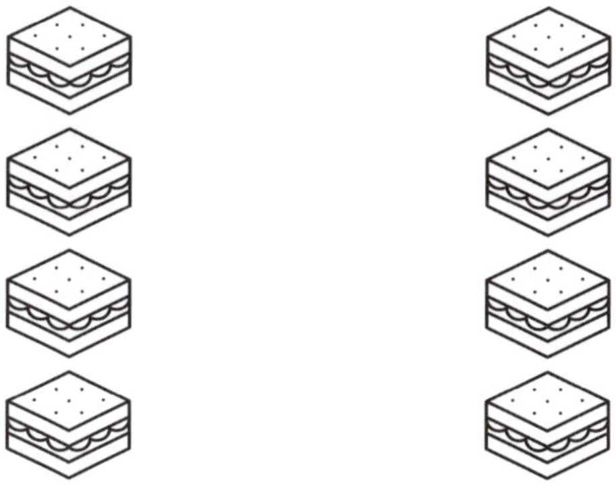

4   > = <   4

Directions: Count the objects in each section. Compare the two numbers in each section. Circle one of these signs > = <. Color the pictures.

DAY 37

Name: _____

 = 5

Remember that a shark ALWAYS wants to eat the bigger number!

Compare Numbers Up to 5

4 > = < 3

2 > = < 2

5 > 1

Directions: Count the objects in each section. Compare the two numbers in each section. Circle one of these signs > = <. Trace the sign. Then, color the pictures.

Name: _____

DAY 38

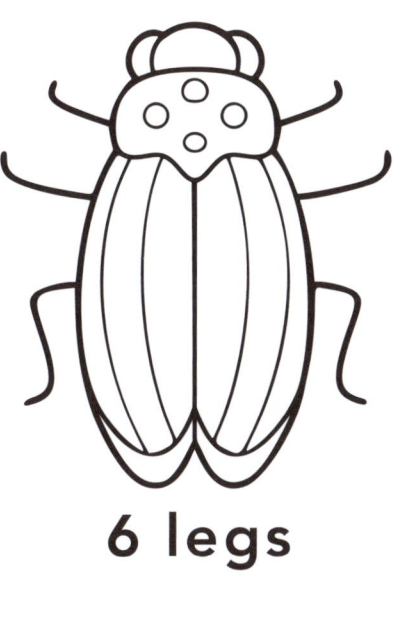
6 legs

six

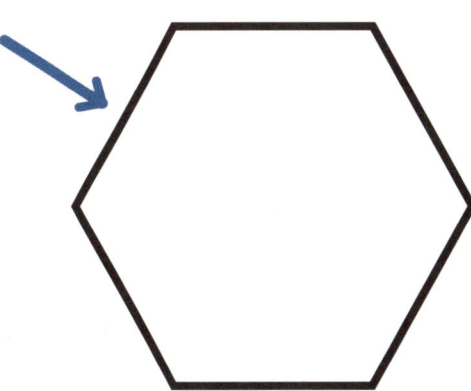
6 sides

6 dots

Time to Draw

Directions: Trace the 6 at least 10 times with your finger. Say its name as you do this. Count the objects in each picture. Color the pictures. Circle each number 6. Then, draw 6 objects.

Name Numbers 6–10

DAY 39

Name: _____

Name Numbers 6–10

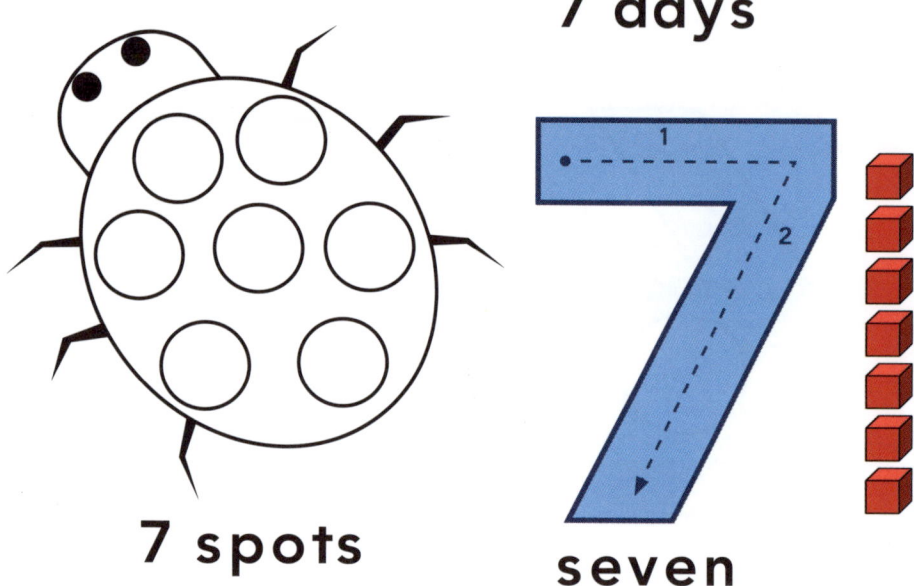

7 days

7 spots

seven

7 colors

Time to Draw

Directions: Trace the 7 at least 10 times with your finger. Say its name as you do this. Count the objects in each picture. Color the pictures. Circle each number 7. Then, draw the number 7 using 7 different colors.

Name: _____

DAY 40

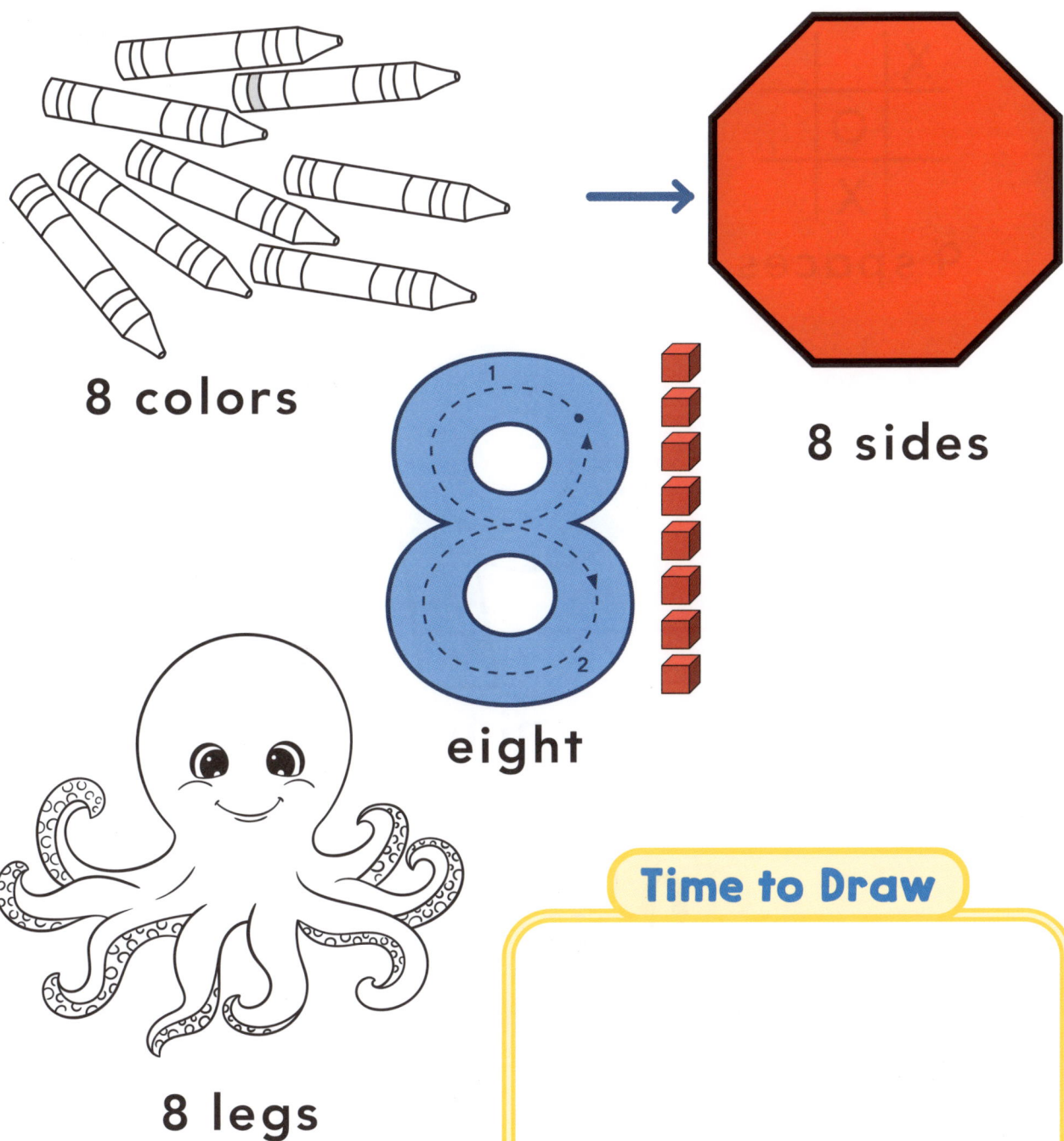

8 colors

8 sides

eight

8 legs

Time to Draw

Directions: Trace the 8 at least 10 times with your finger. Say its name as you do this. Count the objects in each picture. Color the pictures. Circle each number 8. Then, go on a scavenger hunt to look for 8 objects. Draw what you find.

Name Numbers 6–10

DAY 41

Name: _____

9 spaces

9 players

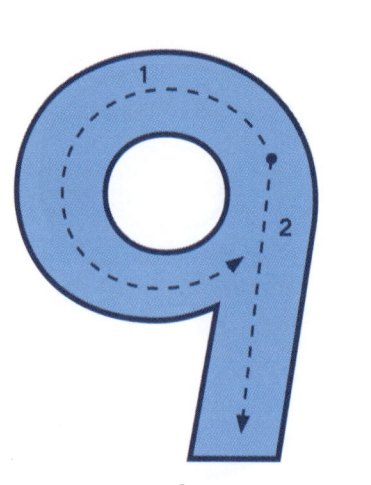

nine

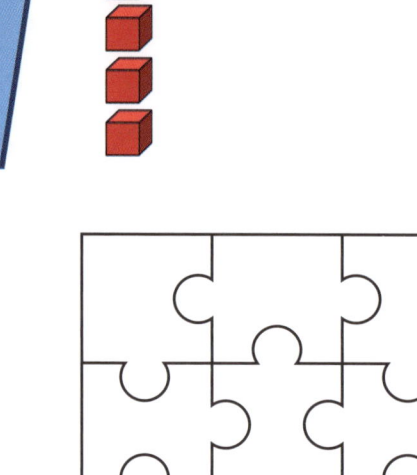

9 pieces

Directions: Trace the 9 at least 10 times with your finger. Say its name as you do this. Count the objects in each picture. Color the pictures. Circle each number 9. Then, find and put boxes around the number 9 on the images.

Name Numbers 6–10

Name: _____

DAY 42

Name Numbers 6–10

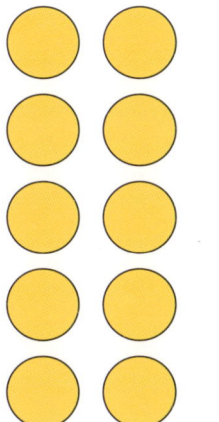
10 counters

10 fingers

 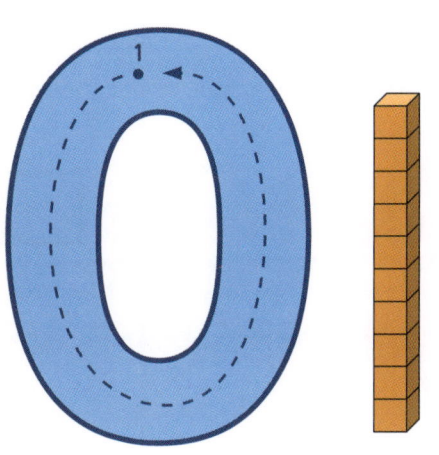

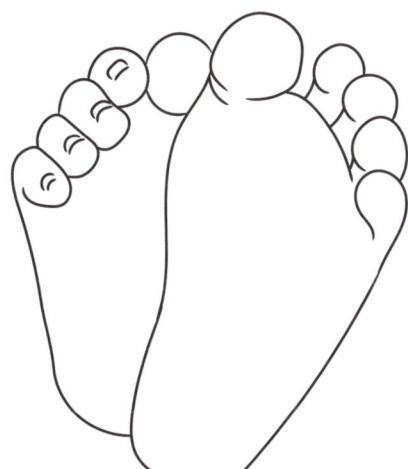
10 toes

Time to Draw

Directions: Trace the 10 at least 10 times with your finger. Say its name as you do this. Count the objects in each picture. Color the pictures. Circle each number 10. Then, draw 10 objects.

DAY 43

Name: _____

Count by Ones to 10

Directions: Count the objects in each row. Write the number of objects in each row. Color the pictures and numbers.

Name: _____

DAY 44

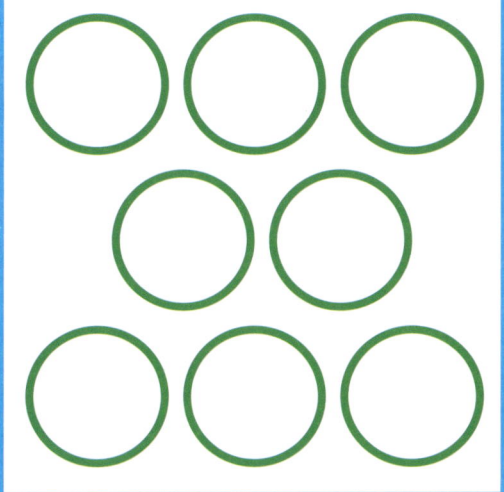  How many?
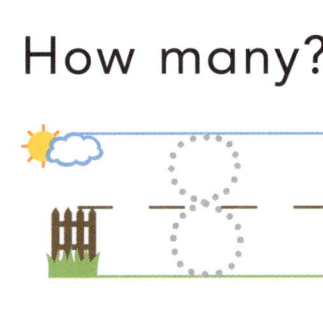

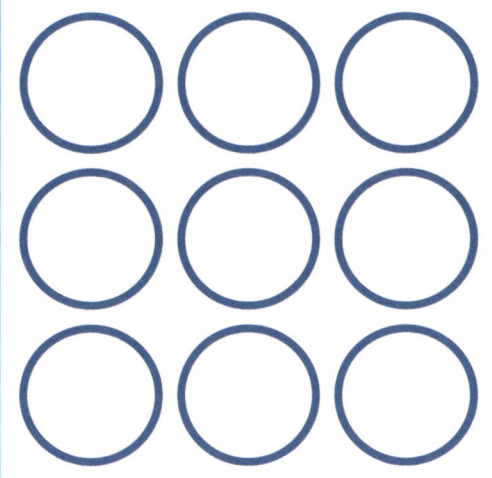 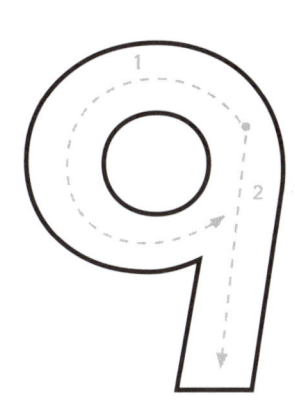 How many?

Count by Ones to 10

Which number is less: 8 or 9?

Directions: Place one small object in each green circle. Count the objects in the green circles. Write the number of objects on the line. Color the green circles. Do the same steps for the blue circles. Then, answer the question.

DAY 45

Name: _____

Count by Ones to 10

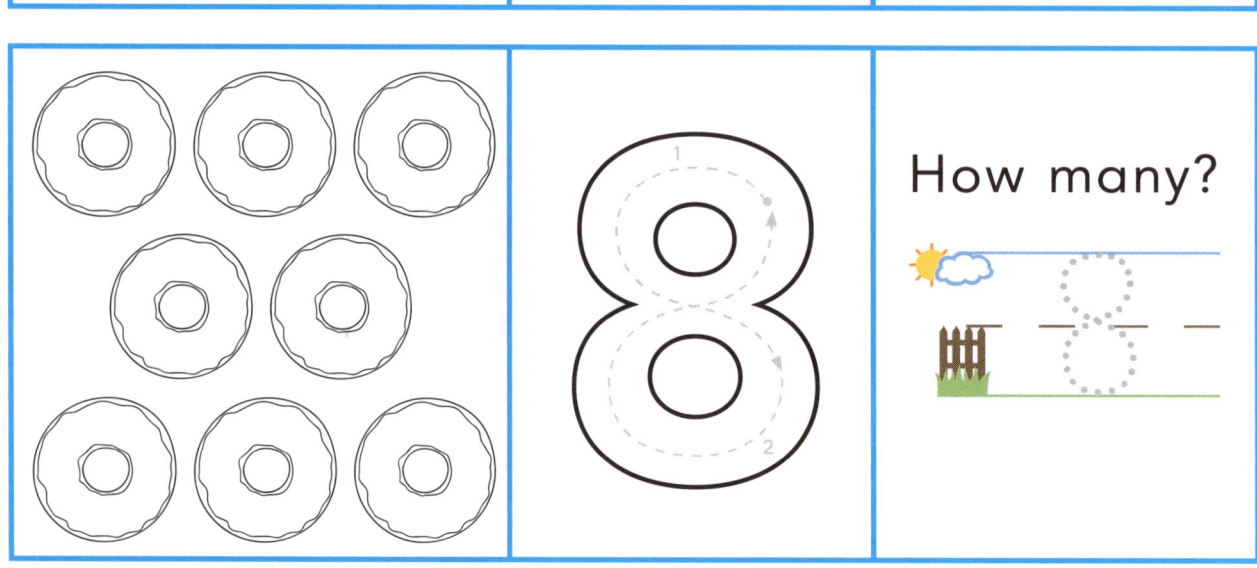

Directions: Count the objects in each row. Write the number of objects in each row. Color the pictures and numbers.

Name: _____

DAY 46

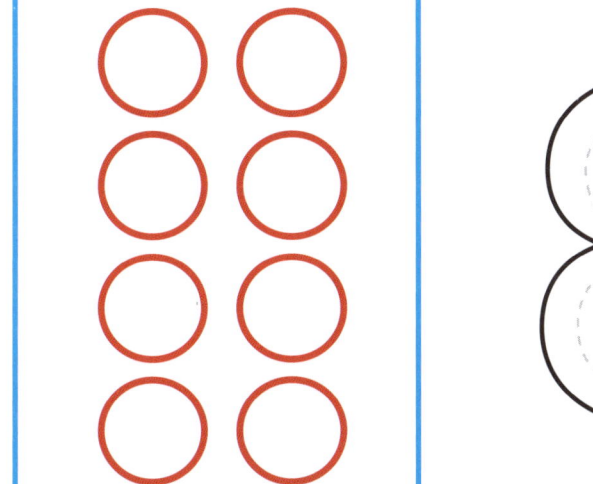

How many?

How many?

Count by Ones to 10

Directions: Place one small object in each red circle. Count the objects in the red circles. Write the number of objects on the line. Color the red circles. Do the same steps for the blue circles. Then, answer the question.

Which number is less: 8 or 10?

DAY 47

Name: _____

Count by Ones to 10

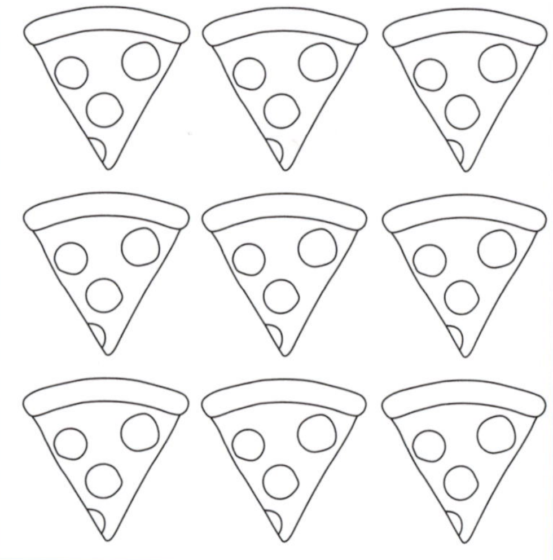

Directions: Count the objects in each row. Write the number of objects in each row. Color the pictures and numbers.

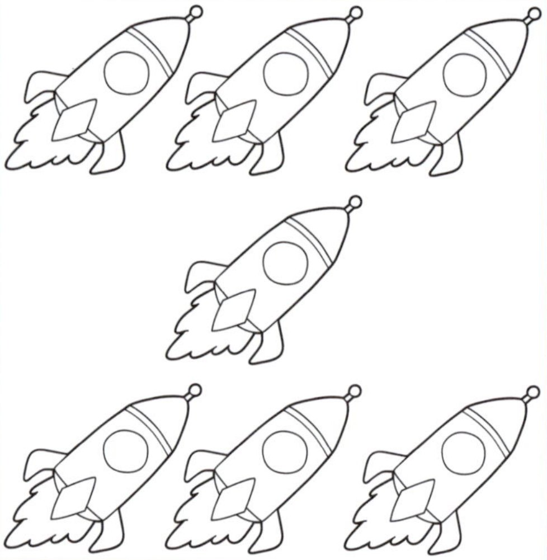

Name: _____

6	10	9	10	8
10	8	10	6	7
8	6	7	9	9
7	9	8	8	10
10	7	10	7	6

How many 6s did you find?

Directions: Find every number 6, and color those squares green. Answer the question. Then, make the number 6 with clay or small objects.

DAY 49

Name: _____

Identify Numbers 6–10

Directions: Find and circle every number 7. Color the drawings of the number 7. Then, make the number 7 with your body.

Name: _____

8	7	8	7	9
6	9	7	6	10
10	7	9	8	8
9	8	10	9	6
7	10	6	10	7

DAY 50

Identify Numbers 6–10

How many 8s did you find?

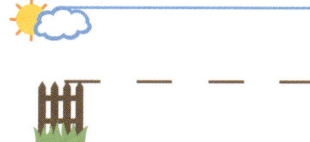

Directions: Find every number 8, and color those squares orange. Answer the question. Then, make the number 8 with clay or small objects.

DAY 51

Name: _____

Identify Numbers 6–10

Directions: Find and circle every number 9. Color the drawings of the number 9. Then, make the number 9 with your body.

Name: _____

8	10	9	6	10
7	8	7	9	9
9	6	10	8	10
10	9	8	7	8
6	7	9	10	7

How many 10s did you find?

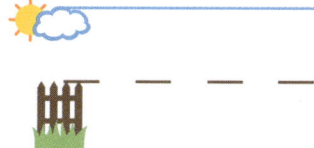

Directions: Find every number 10, and color the squares blue. Answer the question. Then, make the number 10 with clay or small objects.

DAY 53

Write Numbers from 6–10

Name: _____

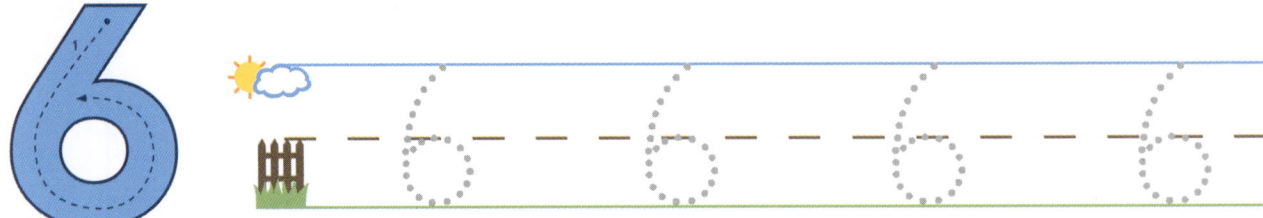
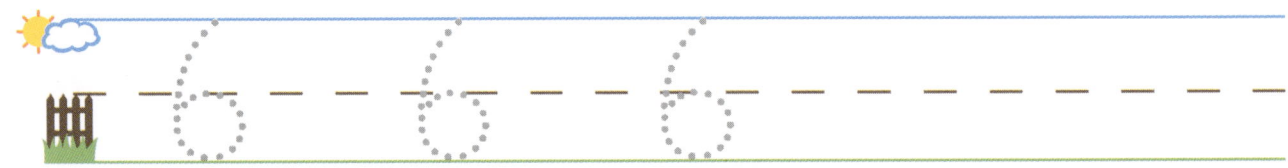
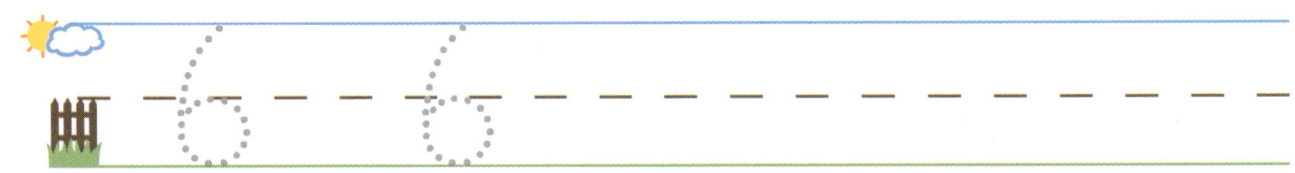

Count on...

Directions: Skywrite the number 6 five times in the air with an invisible pencil. Trace the number 6, and write it on your own. Count the ducks. Then, count on from 3 to fill in the missing numbers. Say each number as you write it.

Name: _____

DAY 54

 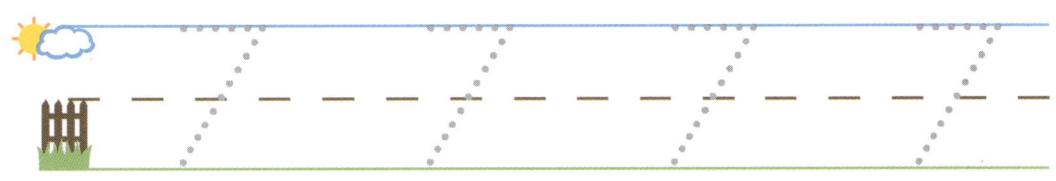

Count on...

   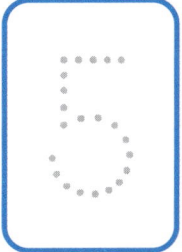  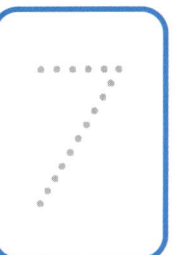

Directions: Skywrite the number 7 five times in the air with an invisible pencil. Trace the number 7, and write it on your own. Count the apples. Then, count on from 4 to fill in the missing numbers. Say each number as you write it.

Write Numbers from 6–10

DAY 55

Name: _____

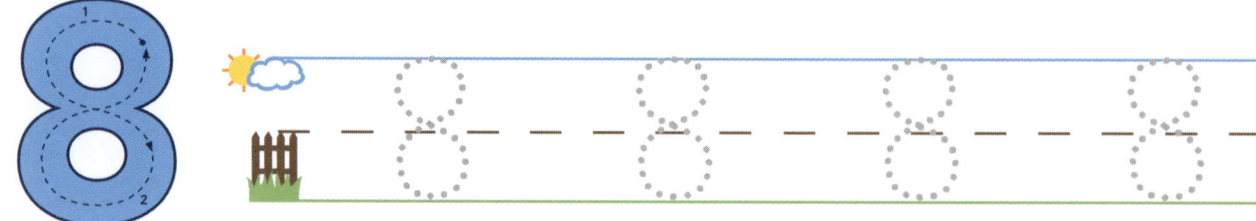

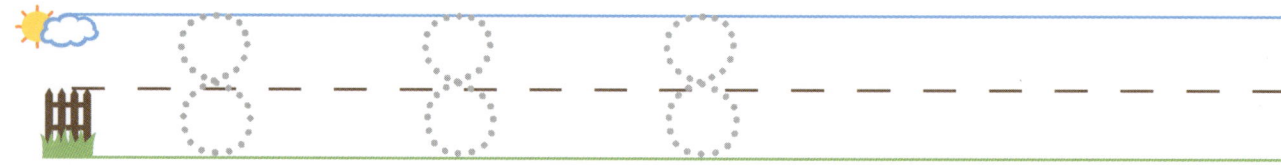

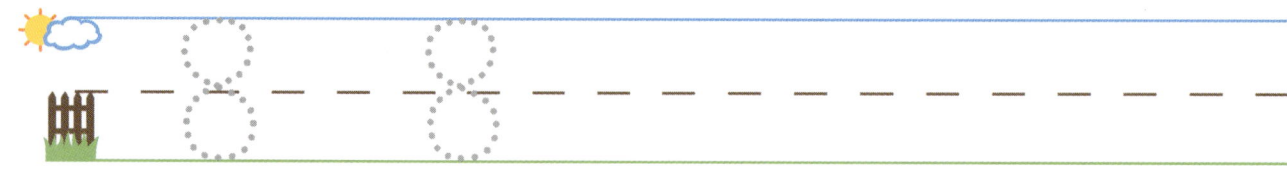

Count on...

Directions: Skywrite the number 8 five times in the air with an invisible pencil. Trace the number 8, and write it on your own. Count the sea stars. Then, count on from 5 to fill in the missing numbers. Say each number as you write it.

Name: _____

DAY 56

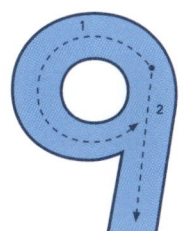 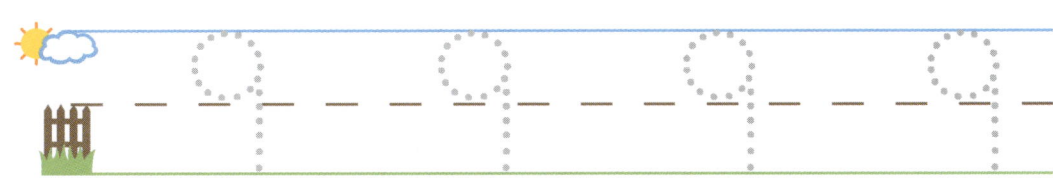

 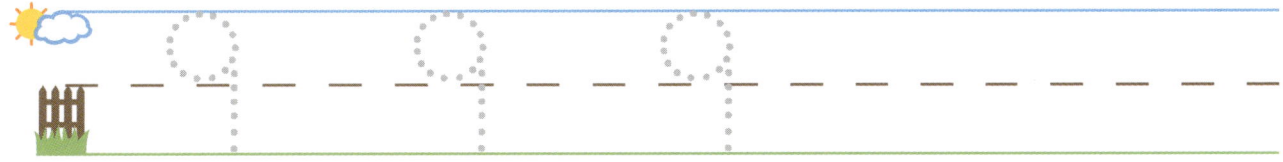

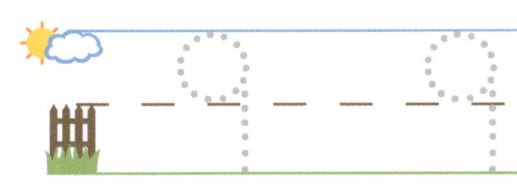

Count on...

Directions: Skywrite the number 9 five times in the air with an invisible pencil. Trace the number 9, and write it on your own. Count the cats. Then, count on from 6 to fill in the missing numbers. Say each number as you write it.

Write Numbers from 6–10

DAY 57

Name: _____

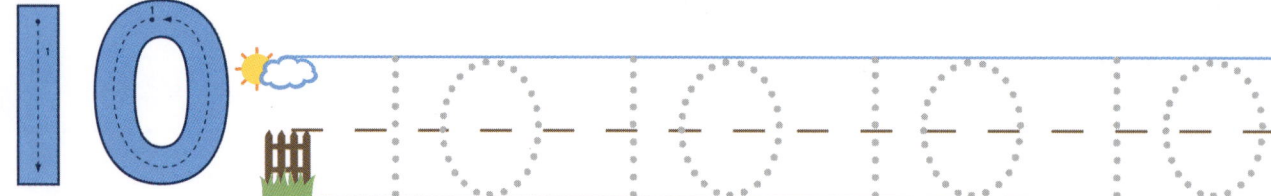

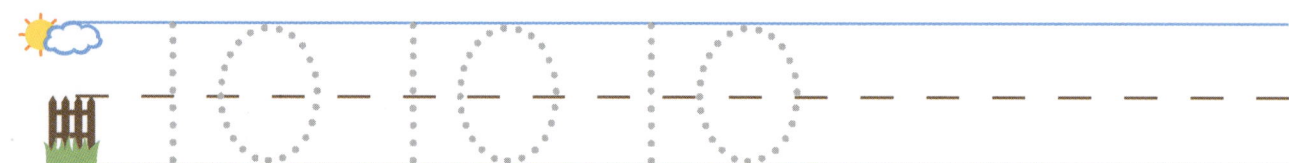

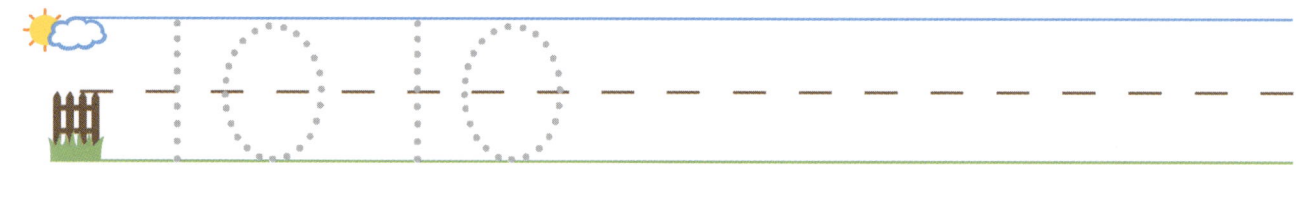

Write Numbers from 6–10

Count on...

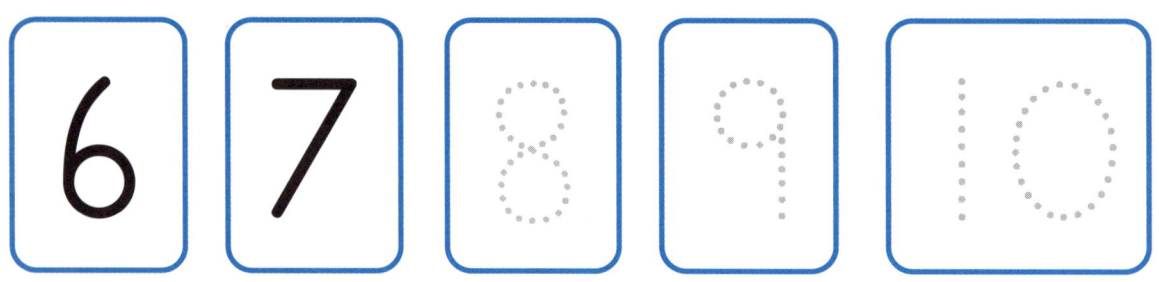

Directions: Skywrite the number 10 five times in the air with an invisible pencil. Trace the number 10, and write it on your own. Count the balls. Then, count on from 7 to fill in the missing numbers. Say each number as you write it.

Name: _____

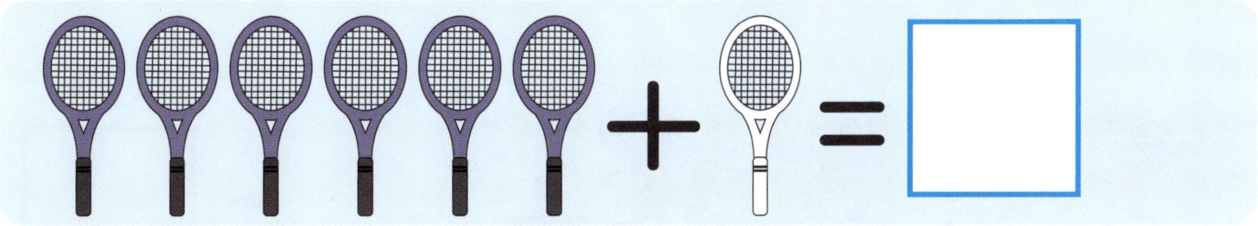

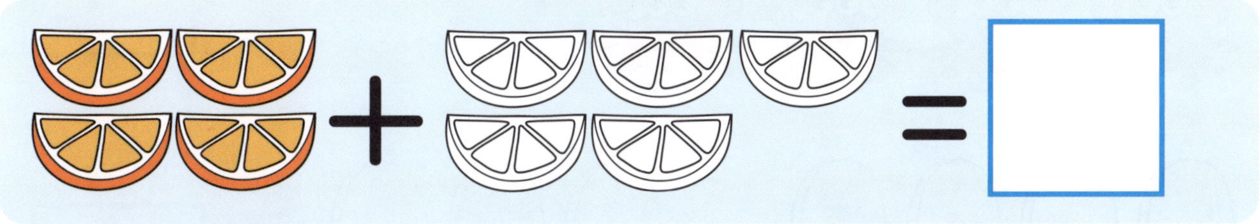

DAY 58

🦖🦖🦖 + 🦖🦖🦖 = 6

🎾🎾🎾🎾🎾🎾 + 🎾 = ☐

🍊🍊🍊🍊 + 🍋🍋🍋🍋🍋 = ☐

🐘🐘🐘🐘🐘 + 🐘🐘🐘 = ☐

Add & Compose Numbers to 10

This is one way to compose 10:

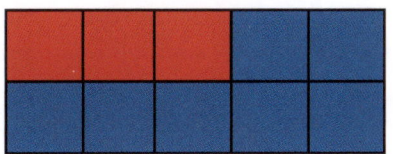

3 and 7 make 10

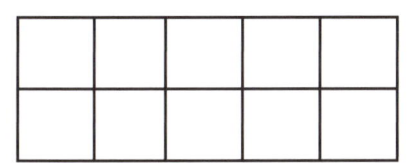

4 and 6 make 10

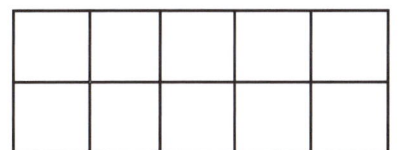

2 and 8 make 10

Directions: Count the objects in each row. Write how many in all in each box. Color the pictures. Then, use two different colors to represent each number as you make the new numbers.

© Shell Education   127443—180 Days of Math   73

DAY 59

Name: _____

Add & Compose Numbers to 10

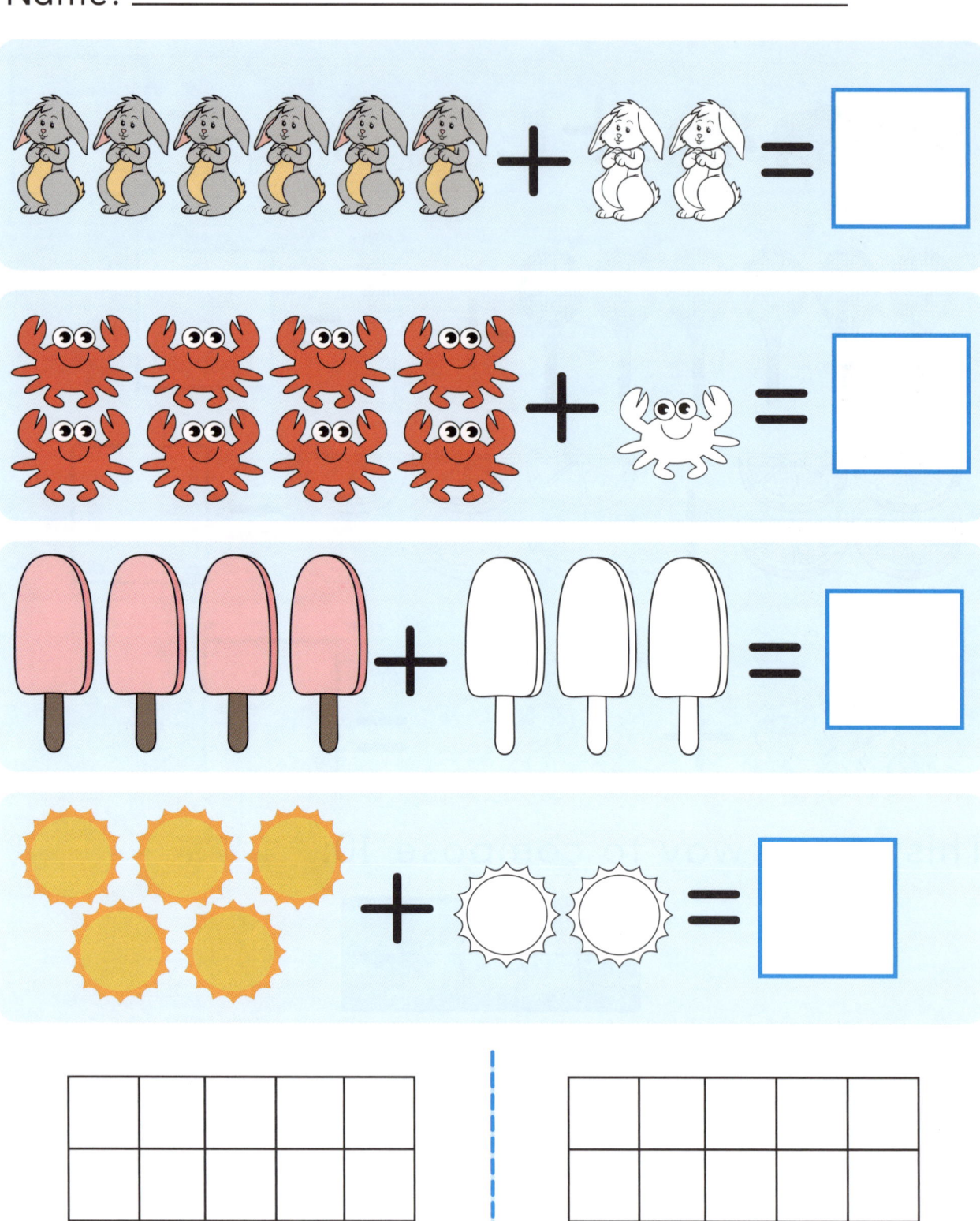

7 and 3 make 10 | 9 and 1 make 10

Directions: Count the objects in each row. Write how many in all in each box. Color the pictures. Then, use two different colors to represent each number as you make the new numbers.

Name: _____

DAY 60

Add & Compose Numbers to 10

 = ☐

 = ☐

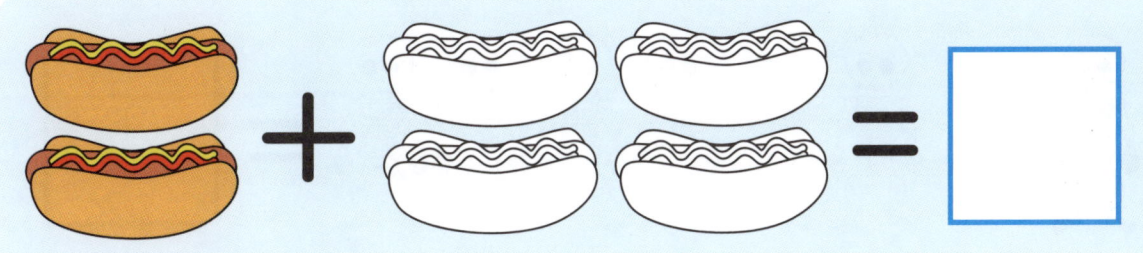 = ☐

 = ☐

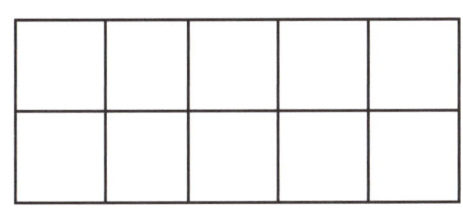

8 and 2 make 10

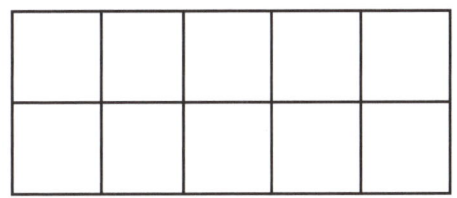

6 and 4 make 10

Directions: Count the objects in each row. Write how many in all in each box. Color the pictures. Then, use two different colors to represent each number as you make the new numbers.

© Shell Education

127443—180 Days of Math 75

DAY 61

Name: _____

Add & Compose Numbers to 10

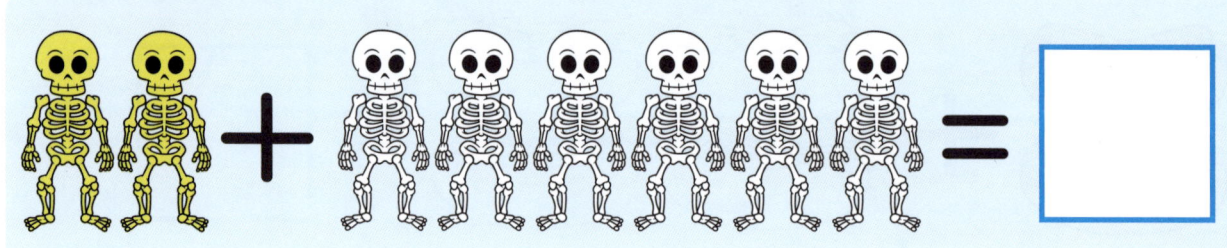

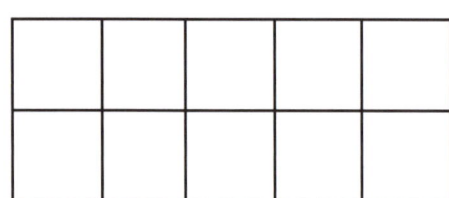

5 and 5 make 10

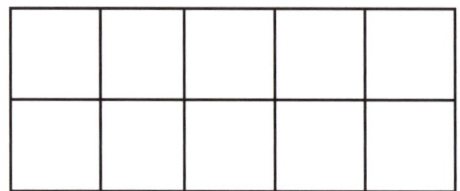

3 and 7 make 10

Directions: Count the objects in each row. Write how many in all in each box. Color the pictures. Then, use two different colors to represent each number as you make the new numbers.

Name: _____

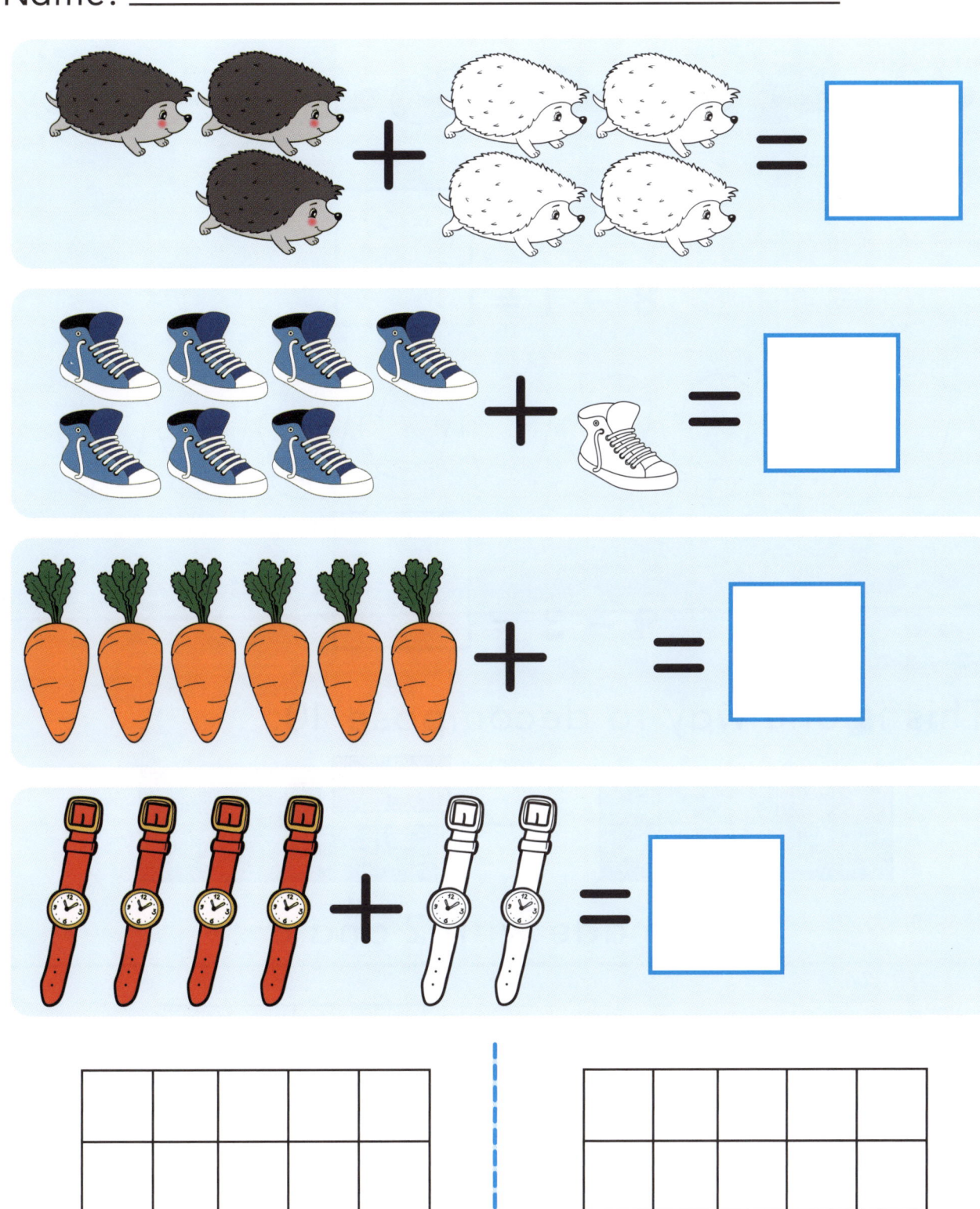

1 and 9 make 10 | 10 and 0 make 10

Directions: Count the objects in each row. Write how many in all in each box. Color the pictures. Then, use two different colors to represent each number as you make the new numbers.

DAY 63

Name: _____

$8 - 1 = \boxed{7}$

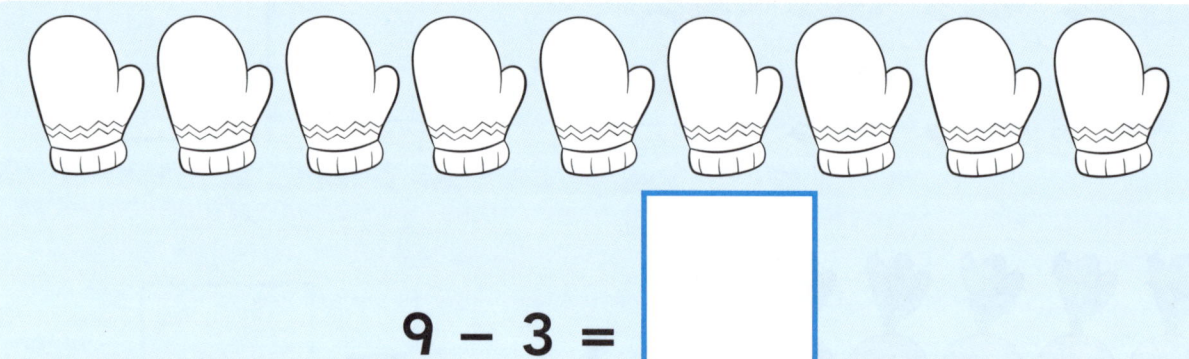

$9 - 3 = \boxed{}$

This is one way to decompose 10:

10 made with 2 and 8

- -

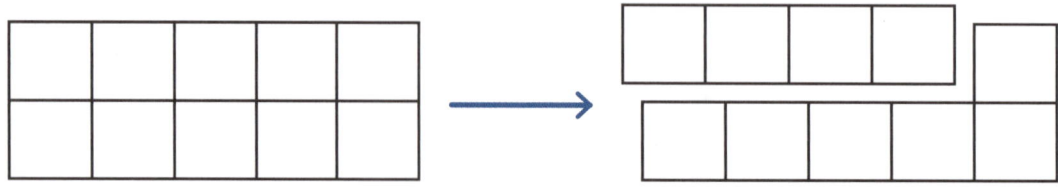

10 made with 4 and 6

Directions: Count the objects in each section. Mark an X on the objects taken away. Color the objects that are left over. Write the amount in each box. Then, use two different colors to show how you decomposed the number 10.

Subtract & Decompose Numbers to 10

Name: _____

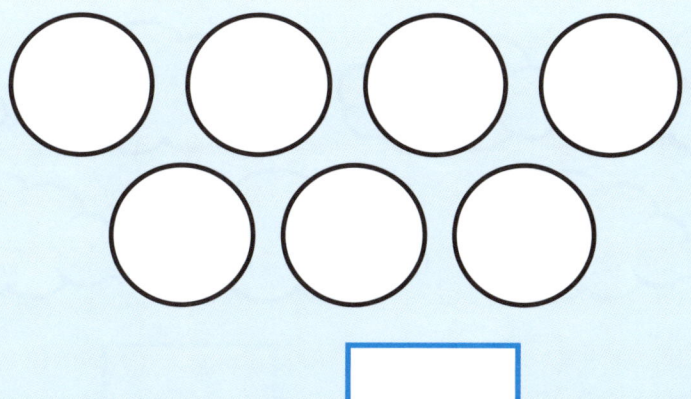

7 − 3 = ☐

8 − 2 = ☐

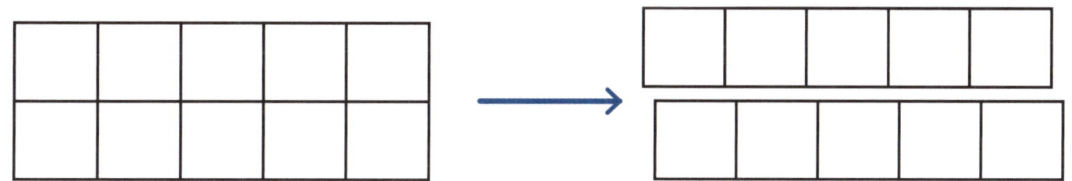

10 made with 5 and 5

Directions: Count the objects in each section. Mark an X on the objects taken away. Color the objects that are left over. Write the amount in each box. Then, use two different colors to show how you decomposed the number 10.

DAY 65

Name: _____

7 − 5 = ☐

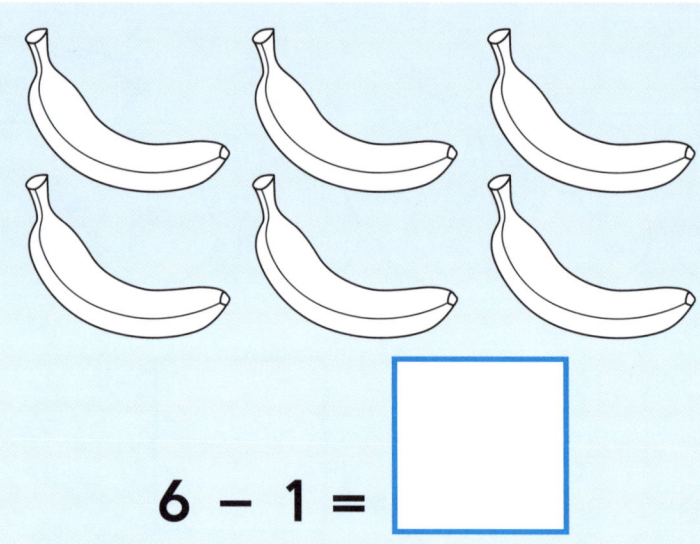

6 − 1 = ☐

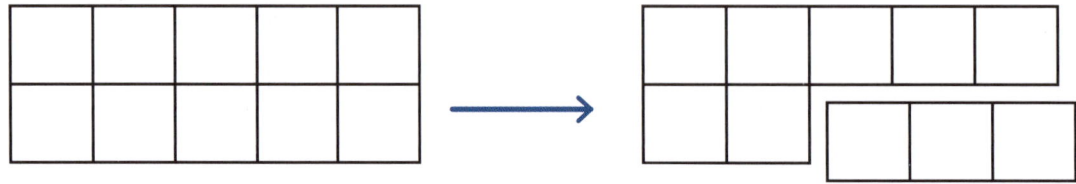

10 made with 7 and 3

Directions: Count the objects in each section. Mark an X on the objects taken away. Color the objects that are left over. Write the amount in each box. Then, use two different colors to show how you decomposed the number 10.

Name: _____

6 − 4 = ☐

8 − 5 = ☐

10 made with 8 and 2

Directions: Count the objects in each section. Mark an *X* on the objects taken away. Color the objects that are left over. Write the amount in each box. Then, use two different colors to show how you decomposed the number 10.

DAY 67

Name: _____

8 − 4 = ☐

7 − 6 = ☐

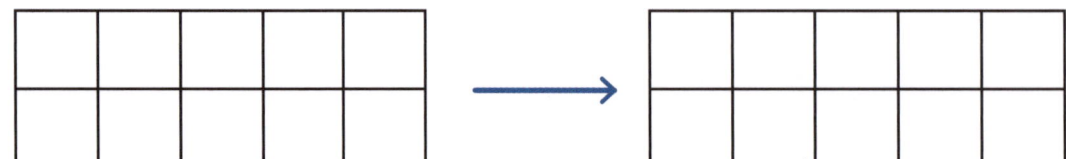

10 made with 10 and 0

Directions: Count the objects in each section. Mark an X on the objects taken away. Color the objects that are left over. Write the amount in each box. Then, use two different colors to show how you decomposed the number 10.

Name: _____

DAY 68

10  7   9 = 9   6  9

Remember that a shark ALWAYS wants to eat the bigger number!

Compare Numbers Up to 10

7 > = (<) 10

8 > = < 8

9 > = < 6

6 > = < 7

Directions: Count the objects in each section. Compare the two numbers in each section. Circle one of these signs > = <. Color the pictures. The first one has been done for you.

DAY 69

Name: _____

 9 > 7   8 = 8   2 < 6

Remember that a shark ALWAYS wants to eat the bigger number!

5   > = <   8

2   > = <   9

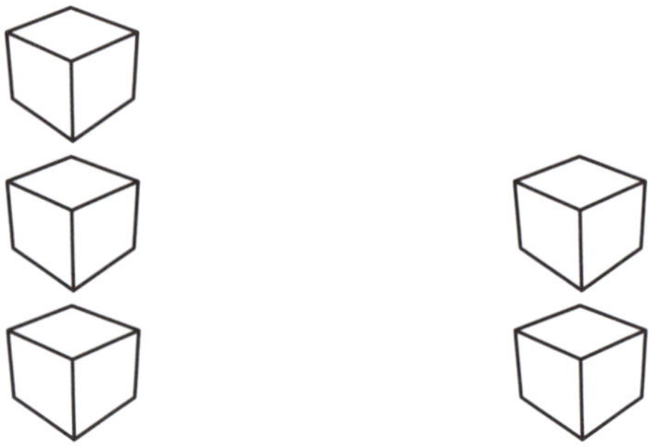

3   > = <   2

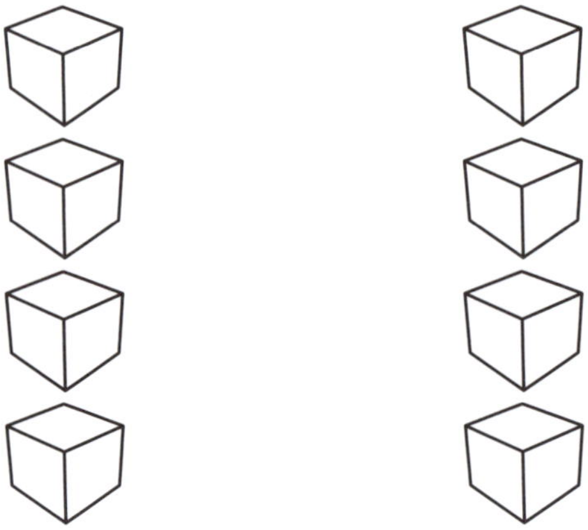

4   > = <   4

Directions: Count the objects in each section. Compare the two numbers in each section. Circle one of these signs > = <. Color the pictures.

Name: _____

DAY 70

 10 > 4   7 = 7   3 < 9

Remember that a shark ALWAYS wants to eat the bigger number!

Compare Numbers Up to 10

6   > = <   10

10   > = <   7

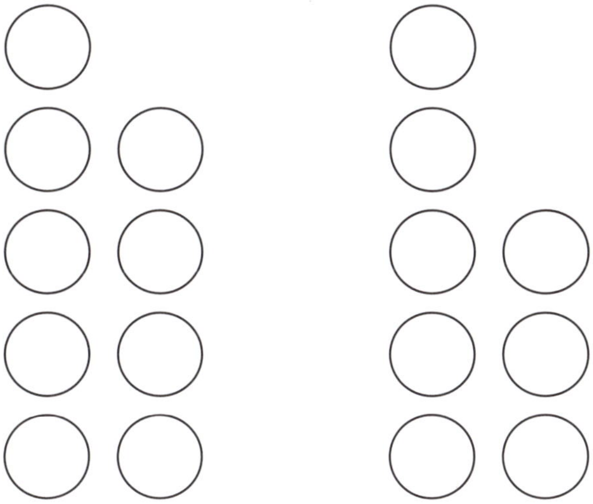

9   > = <   8

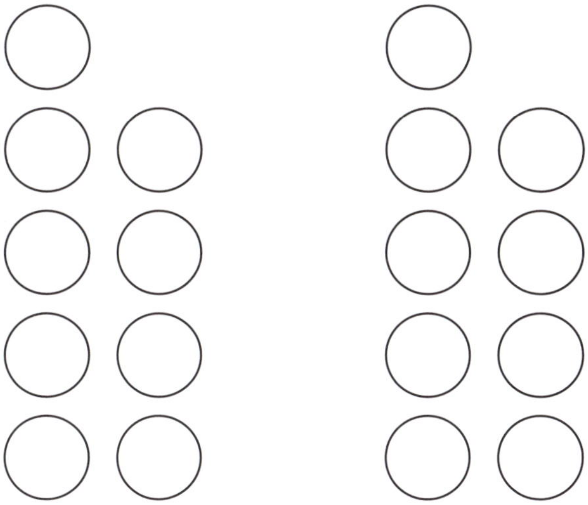

9   > = <   9

Directions: Count the objects in each section. Compare the two numbers in each section. Circle one of these signs > = <. Color the pictures.

DAY 71

Name: _____

6 > 2   10 = 10   7 < 8

Remember that a shark ALWAYS wants to eat the bigger number!

9   > = <   6

8   > = <   9

10 > = <   4

7   > = <   7

Compare Numbers Up to 10

Directions: Count the objects in each section. Compare the two numbers in each section. Circle one of these signs > = <. Color the pictures.

Name: _____

DAY 72

9  6   6 = 6   3  10

Remember that a shark ALWAYS wants to eat the bigger number!

Compare Numbers Up to 10

5 > = < 5

2 > = < 8

4 > = < 9

8 > = < 7

Directions: Count the objects in each section. Compare the two numbers in each section. Circle one of these signs > = <. Color the pictures.

Introducing the Concept

Measurement & Data

Learning All About Length, Weight, and Height!

Now it is time to learn about measurement and data. In this section, students learn about attributes including length, weight, and height. They also learn to measure with nonstandard units of measurement to explore how long, heavy, or high objects are. Students compare objects based on attributes. They continue to investigate numbers by counting and classifying.

What You May Need

- jumbo pencils or short golf pencils
- crayons, colored pencils, etc.

Understanding the Activities

As you work through these pages, here are some ways to further support student learning:

- Discuss the name of each attribute as it is introduced.
- Read directions to students. Follow directions one step at a time, allowing enough time for students to complete each task before moving to the next step in the directions.
- As students write, double-check that they are writing attributes accurately.

Name: _____

DAY 73

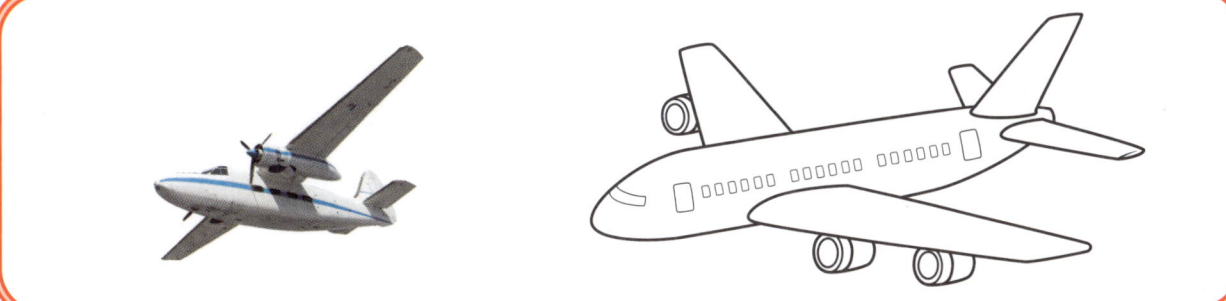

Time to Draw

Directions: Use green to circle the longer object in each box. Use yellow to circle the shorter object in each box. Color the pictures. Then, draw an object that is longer than your shoe.

DAY 74

Name: _____

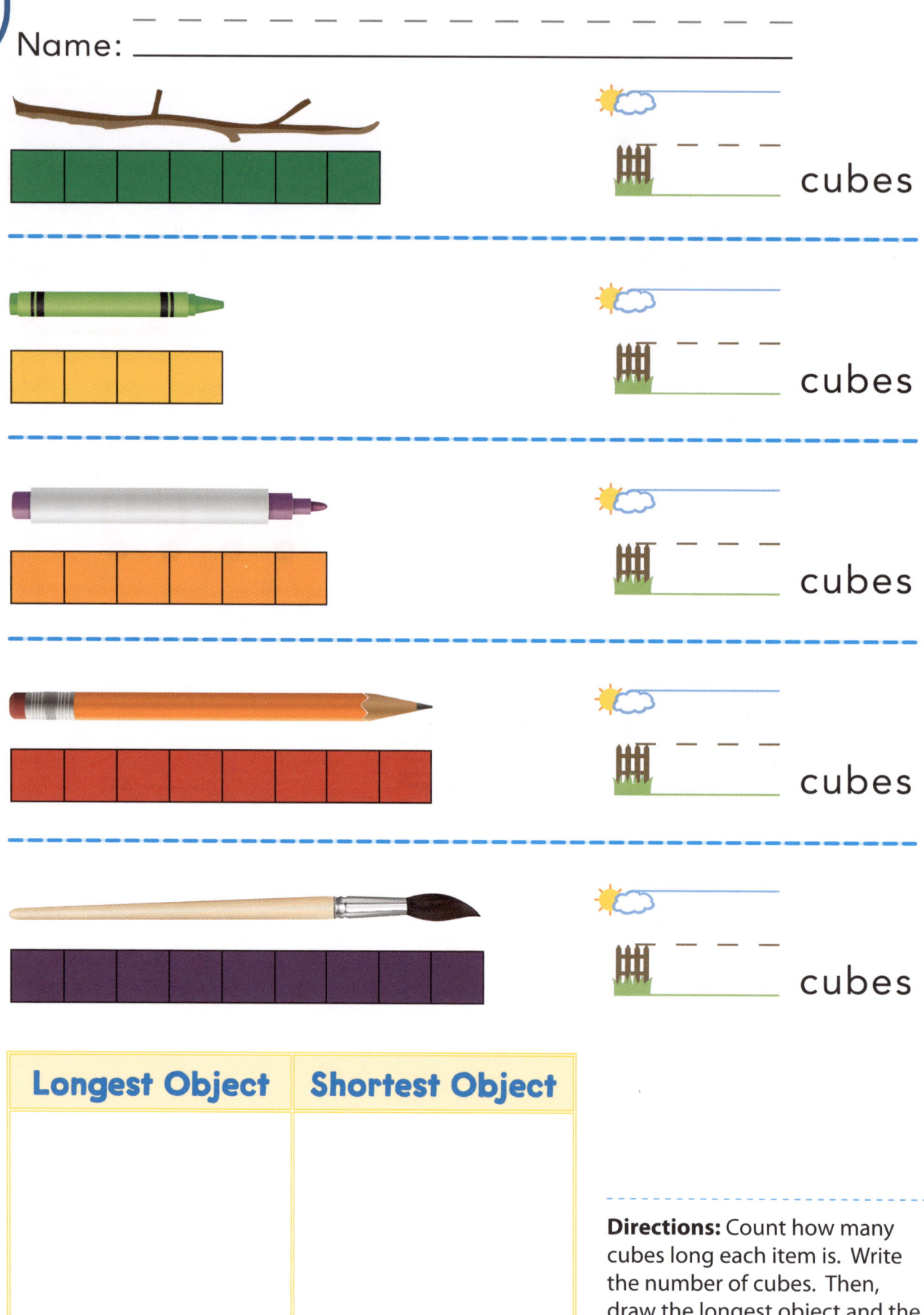

Longest Object	Shortest Object

Directions: Count how many cubes long each item is. Write the number of cubes. Then, draw the longest object and the shortest object.

Name: _____

DAY 75

Attributes

Time to Draw

Directions: Use red to circle the heavier object in each box. Use blue to circle the lighter object in each box. Color the pictures. Then, draw an object that is heavier than a book.

DAY 76

Name: _____

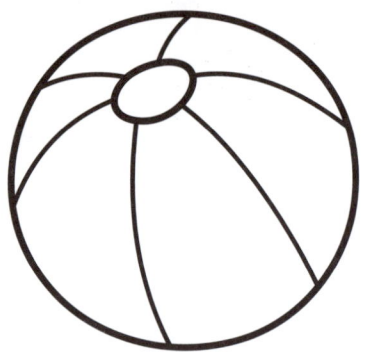

Heaviest Object	Lightest Object

Directions: Circle the objects that are lighter than a glue bottle. Color the pictures. Then, draw the heaviest object and the lightest object.

Name: _____

DAY 77

Attributes

Time to Draw

Directions: Use green to circle the taller object in each box. Use yellow to circle the shorter object in each box. Color the pictures. Then, draw an object that is taller than your shoe.

DAY 78

Name: _____

_____ cubes

_____ cubes

_____ cubes

_____ cubes

Tallest Object	Shortest Object

Directions: Count how many cubes high each item is. Then, write the number of cubes. Color the pictures. Then, draw the tallest object and the shortest object.

Name: _____

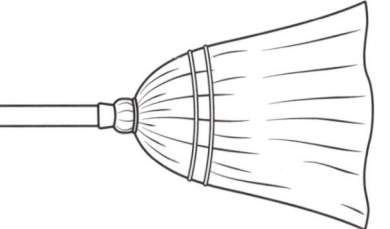 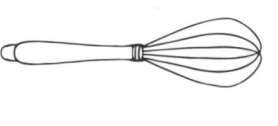

Compare Attributes

Long Object	Short Object

Directions: Circle the shorter object in each pair. Color the pictures. Then, draw one long object and one short object you see in your home.

DAY 80

Name: _____

Compare Attributes

Tall Object	Short Object

Directions: Circle the taller object in each pair. Color the pictures. Then, draw and color one tall object and one short object you see in your neighborhood.

Name: _____

DAY 81

Compare Attributes

Heavy Object	Light Object

Directions: Circle the lighter object in each pair. Color the pictures. Then, draw and color one heavy object and one light object you see in your community.

DAY 82

Name: _____

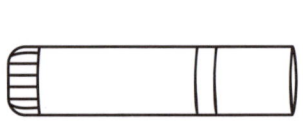 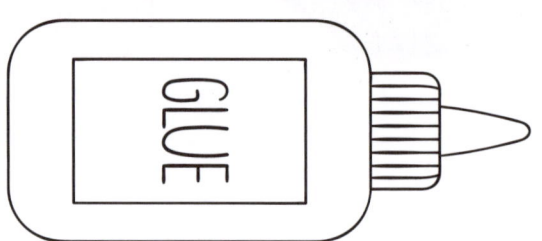

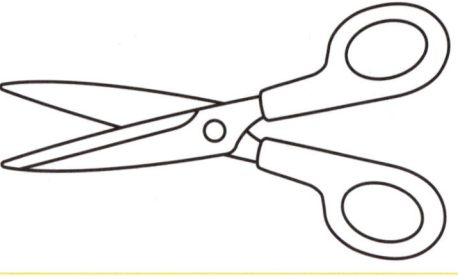 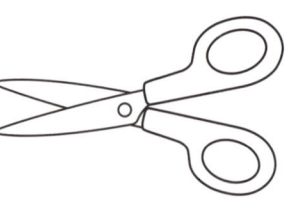

Long Object	Short Object

Directions: Circle the longer object in each pair. Color the pictures. Then, draw one long object and one short object you see in your home.

Name: _____

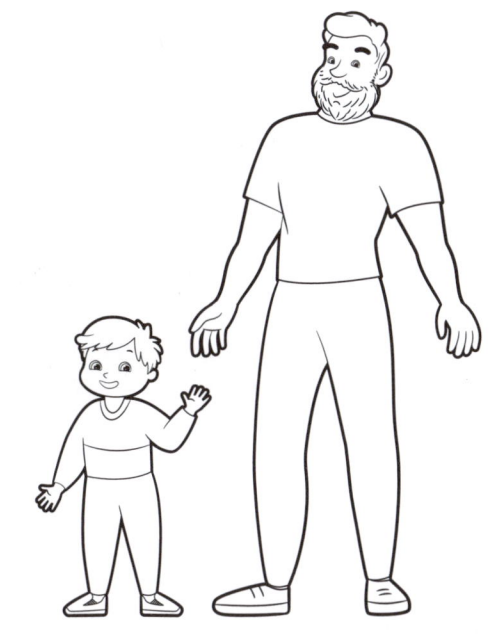

Directions: Circle the shorter person or object in each pair. Color the pictures. Then, draw one tall object and one short object you see in your neighborhood.

Tall Object	Short Object

DAY 84

Name: _____

Classify & Count

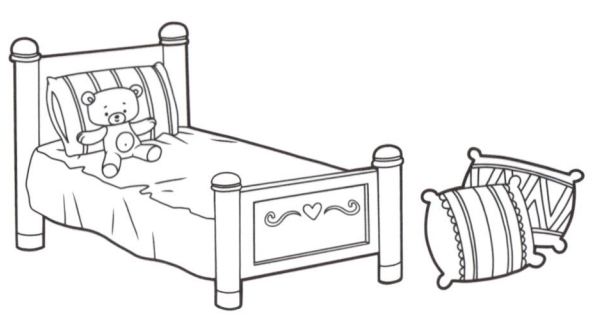

Time to Count

How many heavy objects?

Directions: Circle the heavier object in each pair. Count the number of heavy objects, and answer the question. Then, color the pictures.

Name: _____

DAY 85

Classify & Count

Time to Count

Short Objects	1	2	3	4	5	6	7	8
Long Objects	1	2	3	4	5	6	7	8

Directions: Circle the short objects. Count the number of short objects, and color that number of squares. Count the number of long objects, and color that number of squares with a different color. Then, color the pictures.

DAY 86

Name: _____

Classify & Count

Time to Count

Light Objects	1	2	3	4	5	6	7	8
Heavy Objects	1	2	3	4	5	6	7	8

Directions: Circle the light objects. Count the number of light objects, and color that number of squares. Count the number of heavy objects, and color that number of squares with a different color. Then, color the pictures.

Name: _____

Time to Count

Short Objects	1	2	3	4	5	6	7	8
Tall Objects	1	2	3	4	5	6	7	8

Directions: Circle the short objects. Count the number of shorter objects, and color that number of squares. Count the number of tall objects, and color that number of squares with a different color. Then, color the pictures.

DAY 88

Name: _____

Time to Count

Large Objects	1	2	3	4	5	6	7	8
Small Objects	1	2	3	4	5	6	7	8

Directions: Draw 3 more objects in the frames. Circle all the large objects. Count the number of large objects, and color that number of squares. Then, count the number of small objects, and color that number of squares with a different color.

> Introducing the Concept

Introduction to Numbers 11–20

Learning All About 11–20

Students are introduced to numbers 11 through 20 in this section. They learn the name of each number, how to count up to 20, and how to identify each number from 11 to 20 when it is mixed in with other numbers. Students learn how to write each number from 11 through 20. They learn to add and subtract with numbers up to 20. Students practice composing and decomposing numbers to 20. Finally, they compare numbers up to 20 to see if a number is greater than, less than, or equal to another number.

What You May Need

- jumbo pencils or short golf pencils
- crayons, colored pencils, etc.
- small objects, such as beads or buttons
- small, nonchoking objects for covering-number activities (modeling clay, interlocking cubes, beans, coins, etc.)

Understanding the Activities

As you work through these pages, here are some ways to further support student learning:

- Discuss the names of the numbers as they are introduced.
- Read the directions to students. Follow the directions one step at a time, allowing enough time for students to complete each task before moving to the next step in the directions.
- As students write, double-check that they are writing numbers accurately, following the numbers and arrows. The repetition when learning to write numbers will help them later with fluency.
- If students need extra support with their fine-motor skills, you may want to write the numbers with highlighters or light markers so students can trace over the numbers.
- Discuss the symbols > (greater than), < (less than), and = with students when completing the comparing numbers section. Read the number sentences aloud with students to reinforce what the symbols mean.

DAY 89

Name: _____

11 blocks

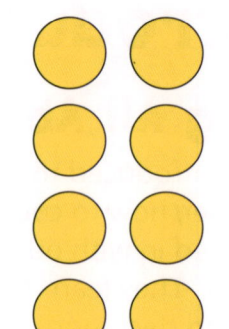
11 counters

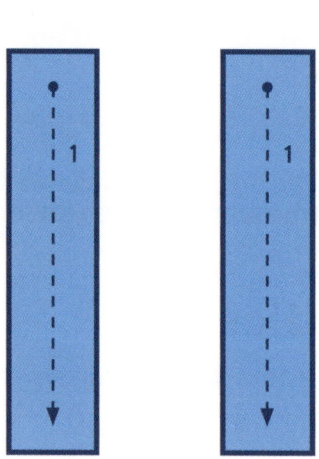
eleven

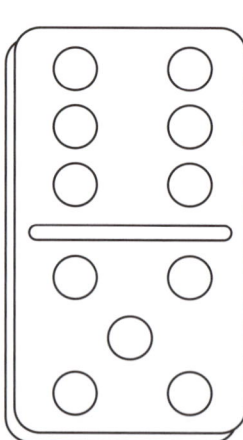
11 dots

Time to Draw

Directions: Trace the 11 at least 10 times with your finger. Say its name as you do this. Count the objects in each picture. Color the pictures. Circle each number 11. Then, draw 11 objects.

Name: _____

DAY 90

Name Numbers 11–15

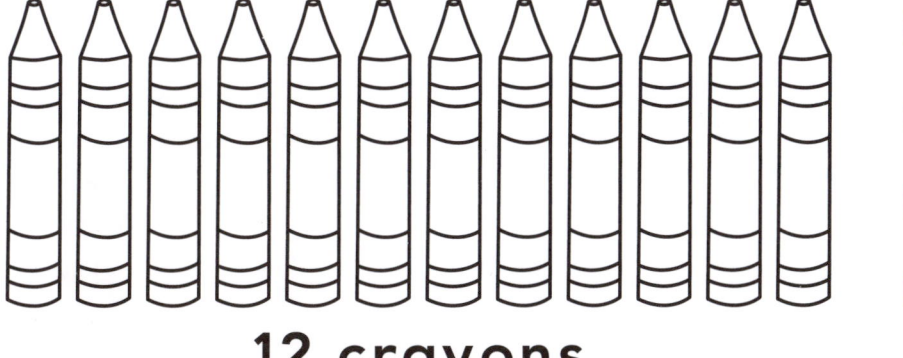

12 crayons

12 counters

twelve

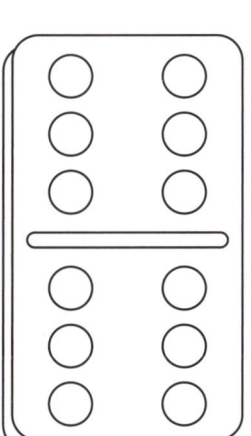

12 dots

Time to Draw

Directions: Trace the 12 at least 10 times with your finger. Say its name as you do this. Count the objects in each picture. Color the pictures. Circle each number 12. Then, draw 12 objects.

DAY 91

Name: _____

13 cars

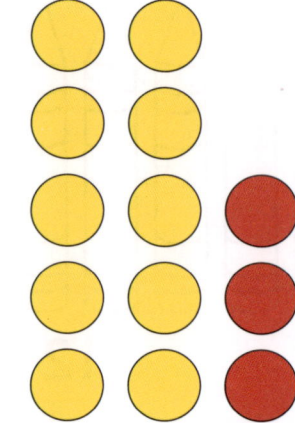
13 counters

thirteen

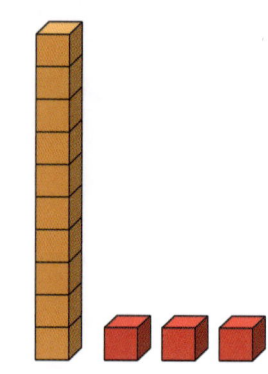

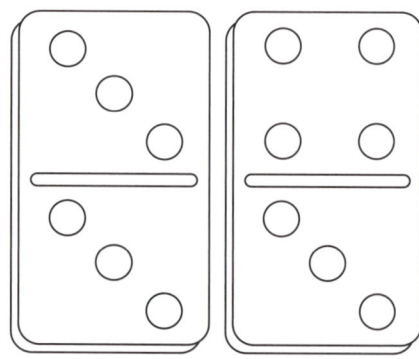
13 dots

Time to Draw

Directions: Trace the 13 at least 10 times with your finger. Say its name as you do this. Count the objects in each picture. Color the pictures. Circle each number 13. Then, go on a scavenger hunt to look for 13 objects. Draw what you find.

Name: _____

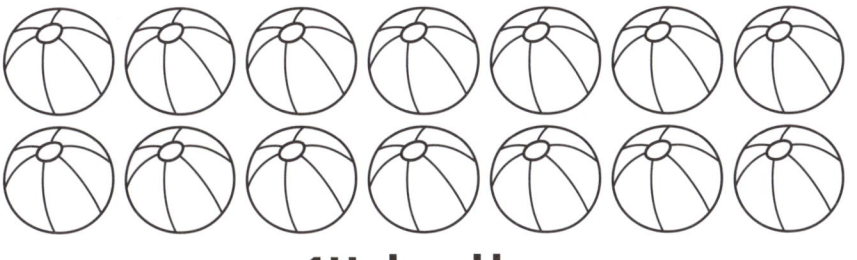
14 balls

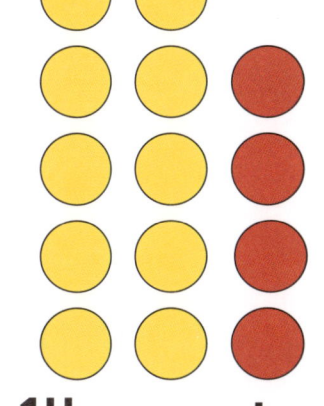
14 counters

14

fourteen

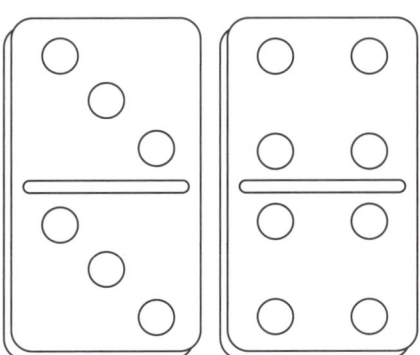
14 dots

Directions: Trace the 14 at least 10 times with your finger. Say its name as you do this. Count the objects in each picture. Color the pictures. Circle each number 14. Then, find and put a box around the number 14 in the images.

DAY 92

Name Numbers 11–15

DAY 93

Name: _____

15 bunnies

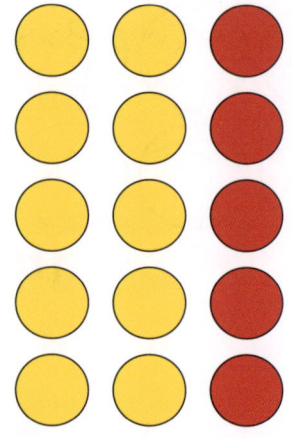
15 counters

fifteen

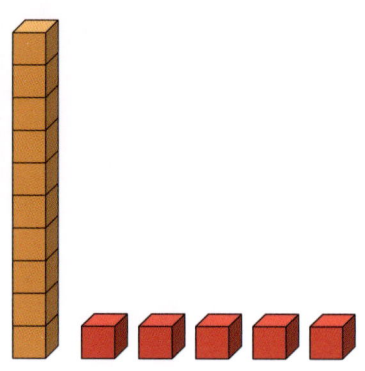

Time to Draw

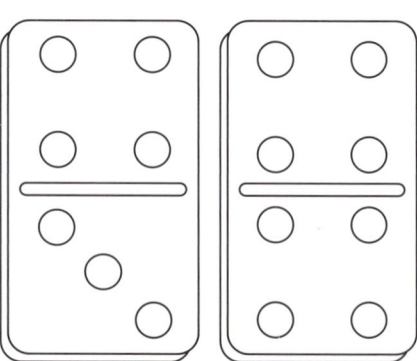
15 dots

Directions: Trace the 15 at least 10 times with your finger. Say its name as you do this. Count the objects in each picture. Color the pictures. Circle each number 15. Then, draw 15 objects.

Name Numbers 11–15

Name: _____

DAY 94

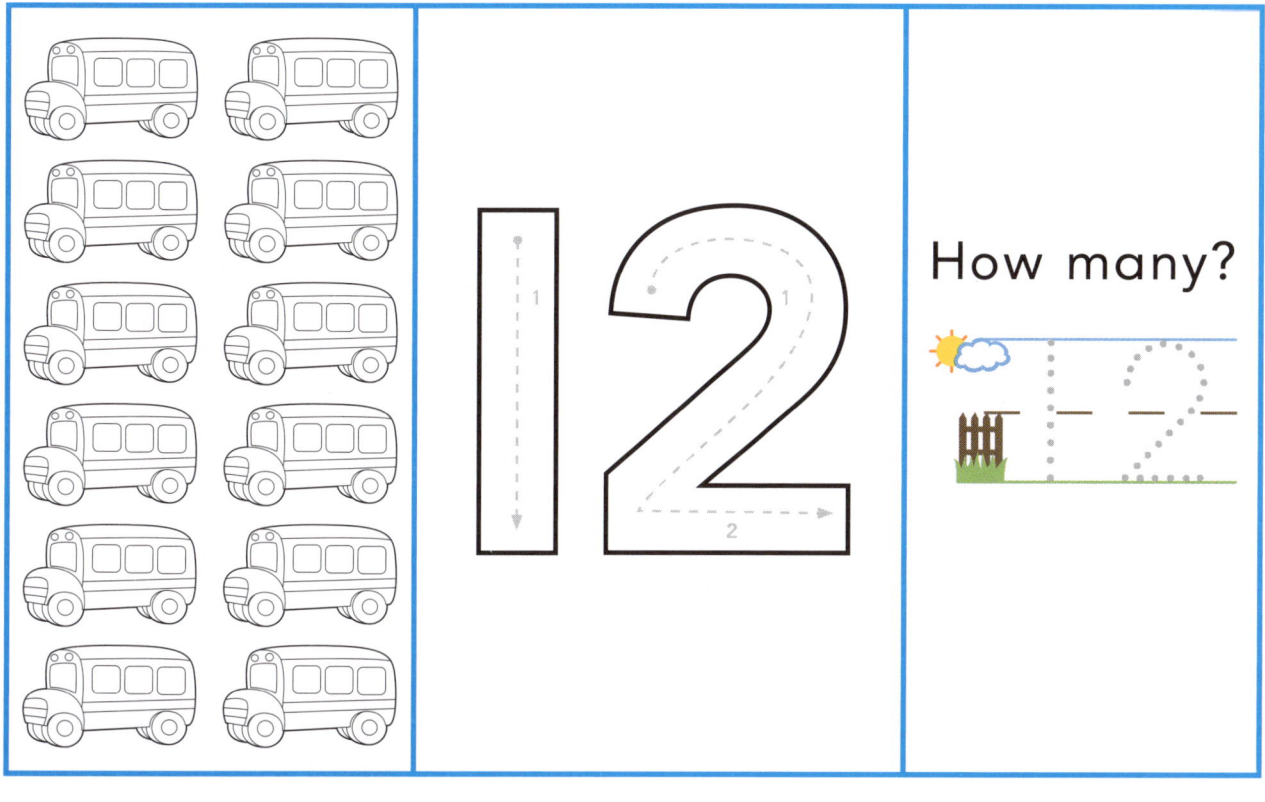

Directions: Count the objects in each row. Write the number of objects in each row. Color the pictures and numbers.

Count by Ones to 15

DAY 95

Name: _____

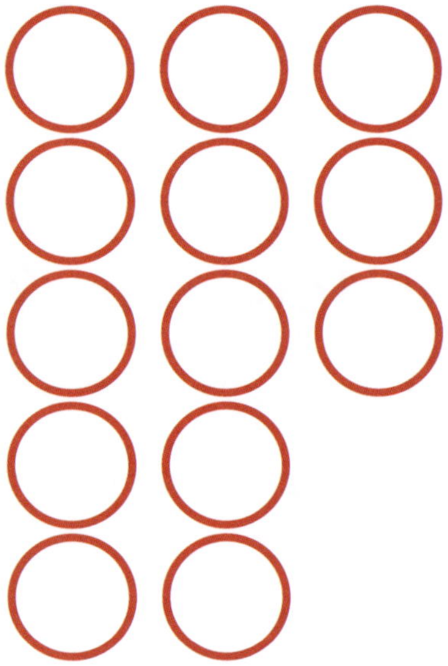

How many?

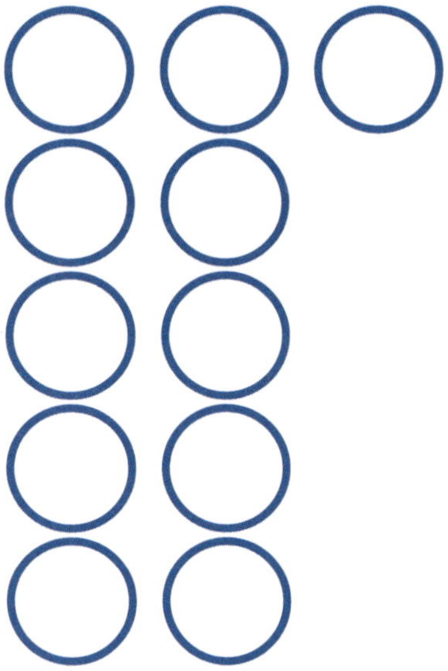

How many?

Which number is less: 11 or 13?

Directions: Place one small object in each red circle. Count the objects in the red circles. Write the number of objects one the line. Color the red circles. Do the same steps for the blue circles. Then, answer the question.

Name: _____

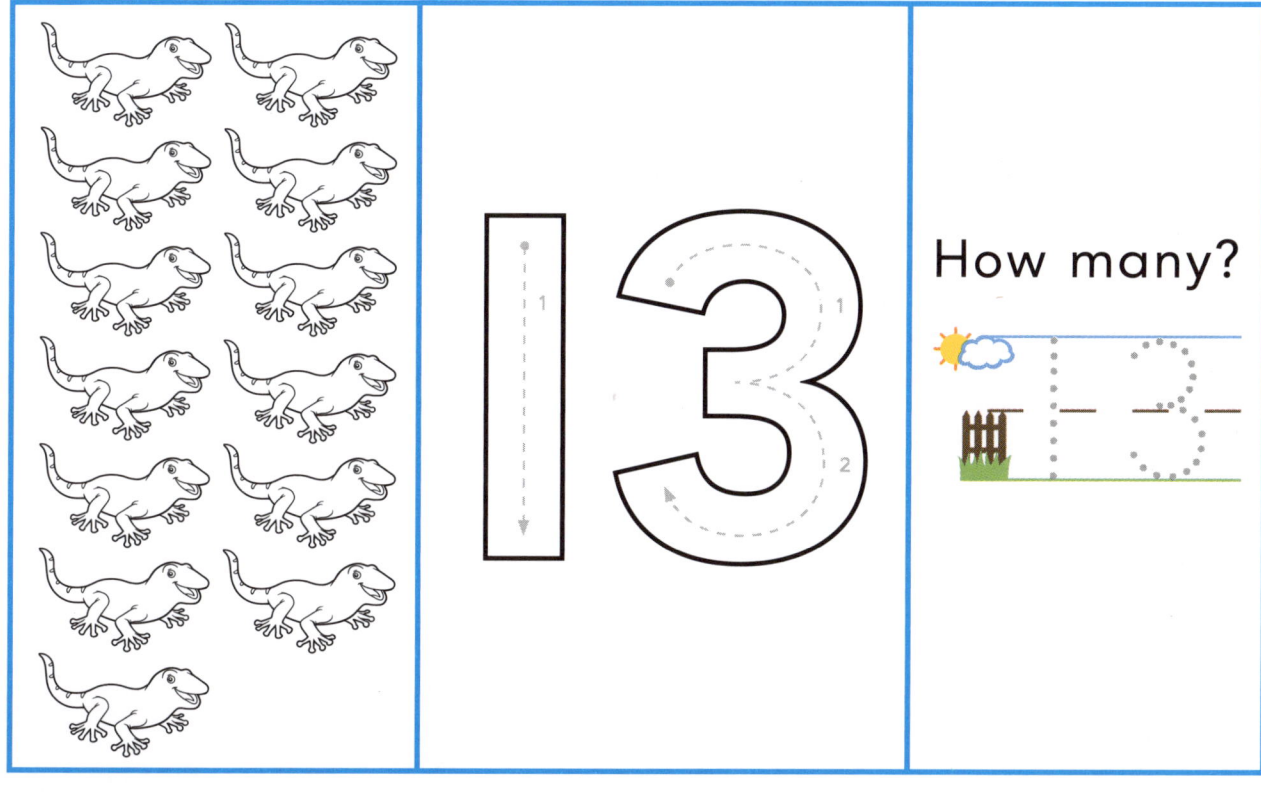

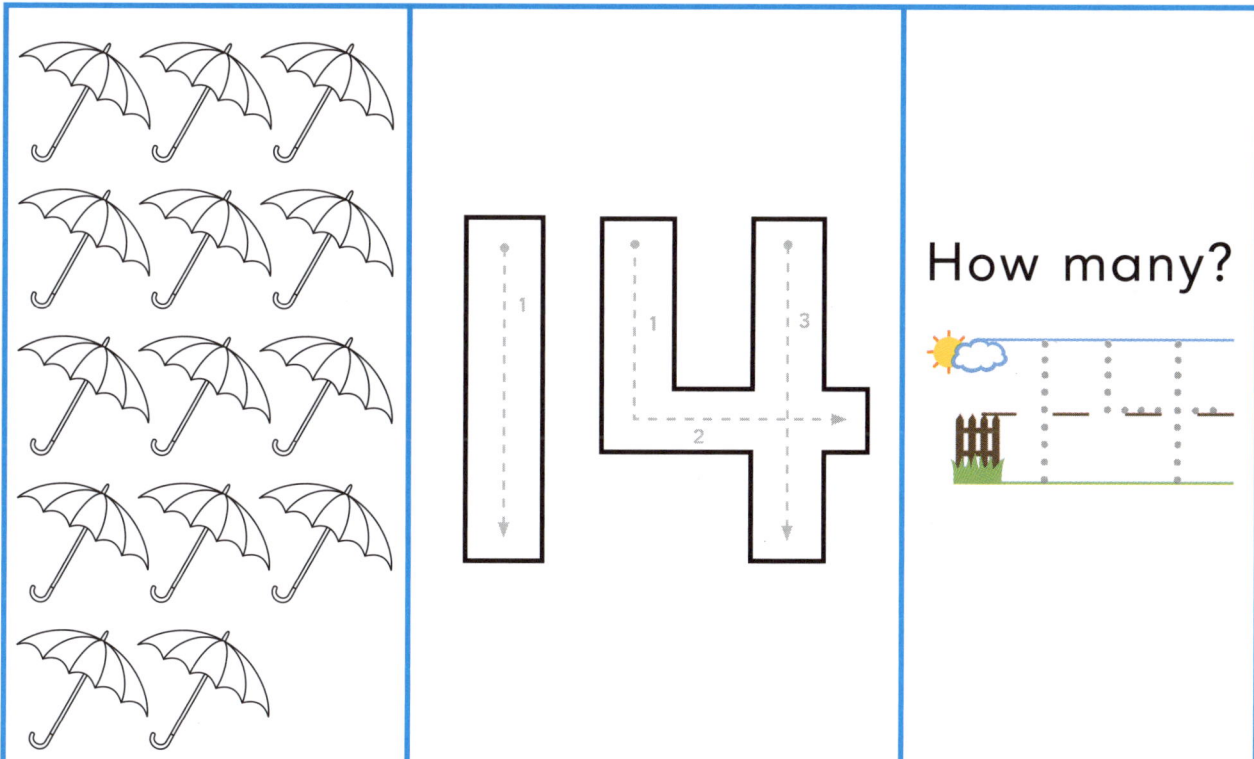

Directions: Count the objects in each row. Write the number of objects in each row. Color the pictures and numbers.

DAY 97

Name: _____

Count by Ones to 15

[15 green circles arranged in 5 rows of 3]

15

How many? _____

[10 blue circles arranged in 5 rows of 2]

10

How many? _____

Which number is more: 10 or 15?

_____

Directions: Place one small object in each green circle. Count the objects in the green circles. Write the number of objects on the line. Color the green circles. Do the same steps for the blue circles. Then, answer the question.

Name: _____

DAY 98

Directions: Count the objects in each row. Write the number of objects in each row. Color the pictures and numbers.

Count by Ones to 15

DAY 99

Name: _____

Identify Numbers 11–15

11	15	14	15	13
15	13	15	11	12
13	11	12	14	14
12	14	11	13	15
14	12	14	12	11

How many 11s did you find?

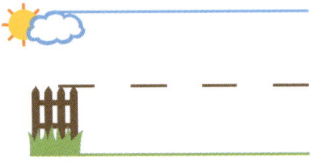

Directions: Find every number 11, and color those squares yellow. Answer the question. Then, make the number 11 with clay or small objects.

Name: _____

DAY 100

Identify Numbers 11–15

Directions: Find and circle every number 12. Color the drawings of the number 12. Then, skywrite the number 12 at least five times in the air using an invisible pencil. Hop 12 times.

DAY 101

Name: _____

Identify Numbers 11–15

13	12	15	12	14
11	14	13	15	15
15	12	14	11	13
14	13	15	14	11
12	15	11	13	12

How many 13s did you find?

Directions: Find every number 13, and color those squares orange. Answer the question. Then, make the number 13 with clay or small objects.

Name: _____

DAY 102

Identify Numbers 11–15

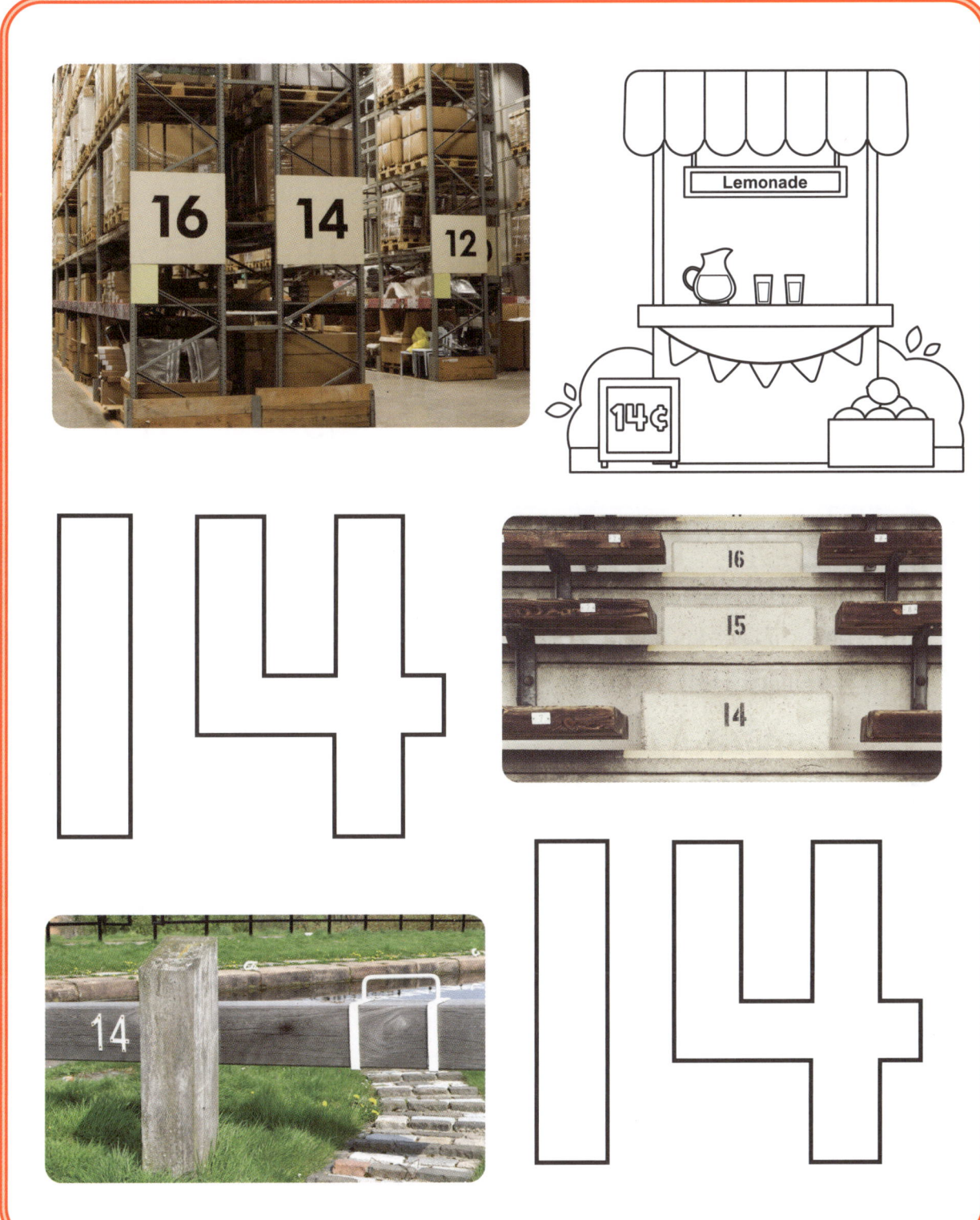

Directions: Find and circle every number 14. Color the drawings of the number 14. Then, skywrite the number 14 at least five times in the air using an invisible pencil. Jump 14 times.

DAY 103

Identify Numbers 11–15

Name: _____

11	15	13	11	12
12	13	12	14	15
14	11	15	13	11
15	14	13	12	13
11	12	14	15	12

How many 15s did you find?

Directions: Find every number 15, and color those squares red. Answer the question. Then, make the number 15 with clay or small objects.

Name: _____

  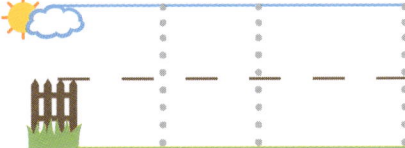

Count on...

8   9   10

Directions: Skywrite the number 11 five times in the air with an invisible pencil. Trace the number 11, and write it on your own. Count the sunflowers. Then, count on by ones to fill in the missing number.

DAY 104

Write Numbers from 11–15

DAY 105

Write Numbers from 11–15

Name: _____

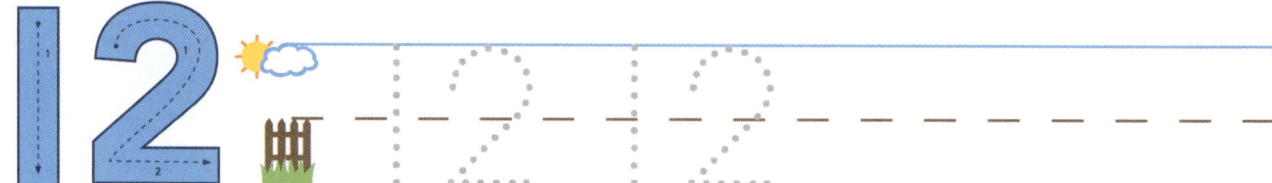

Count on...

9   10   11   ____

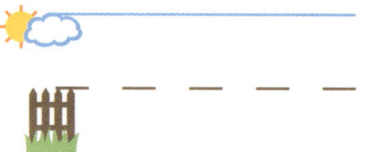

Directions: Skywrite the number 12 five times in the air with an invisible pencil. Trace the number 12, and write it on your own. Count each cactus. Then, count on by ones to fill in the missing number.

Name: _____

DAY 106

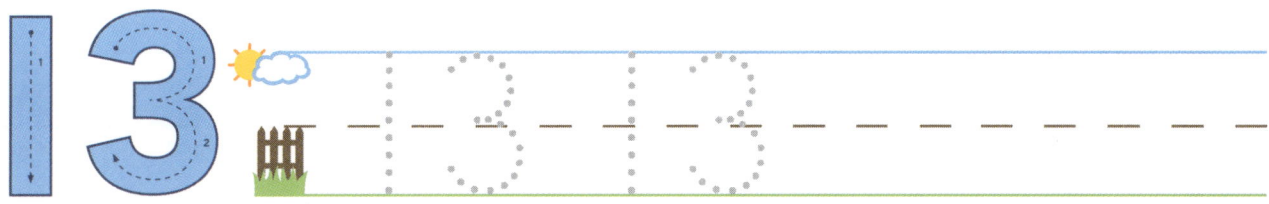

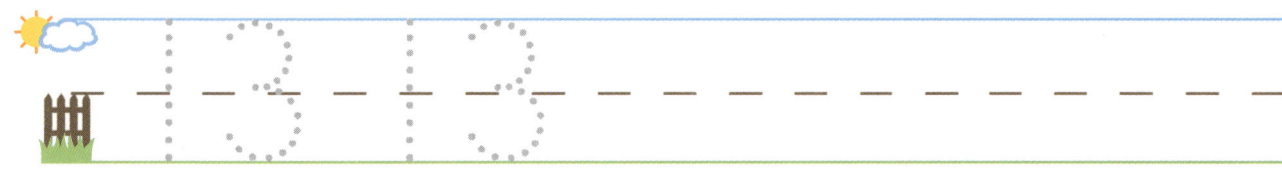

Count on...

10 11 12 ___

Directions: Skywrite the number 13 five times in the air with an invisible pencil. Trace the number 13, and write it on your own. Count the ladybugs. Then, count on by ones to fill in the missing number.

Write Numbers from 11–15

DAY 107

Name: _____

Write Numbers from 11–15

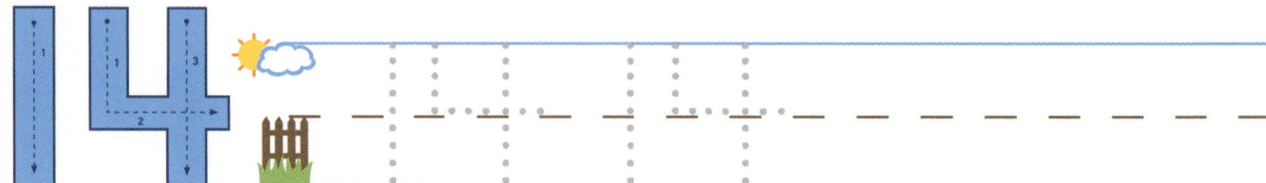

Count on...

11   12   13   ___

Directions: Skywrite the number 14 five times in the air with an invisible pencil. Trace the number 14, and write it on your own. Count the bees. Then, count on by ones to fill in the missing number.

124   127443—180 Days of Math   © Shell Education

Name: _____

DAY 108

Write Numbers from 11–15

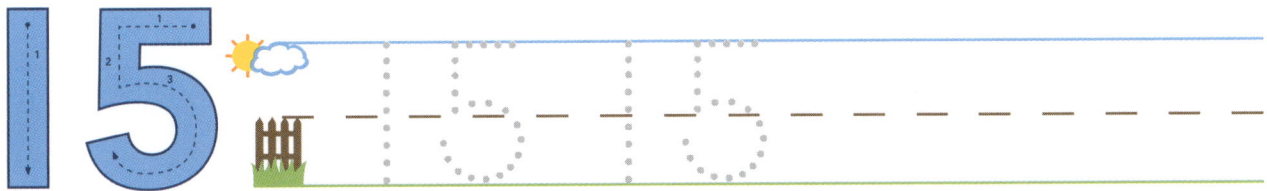

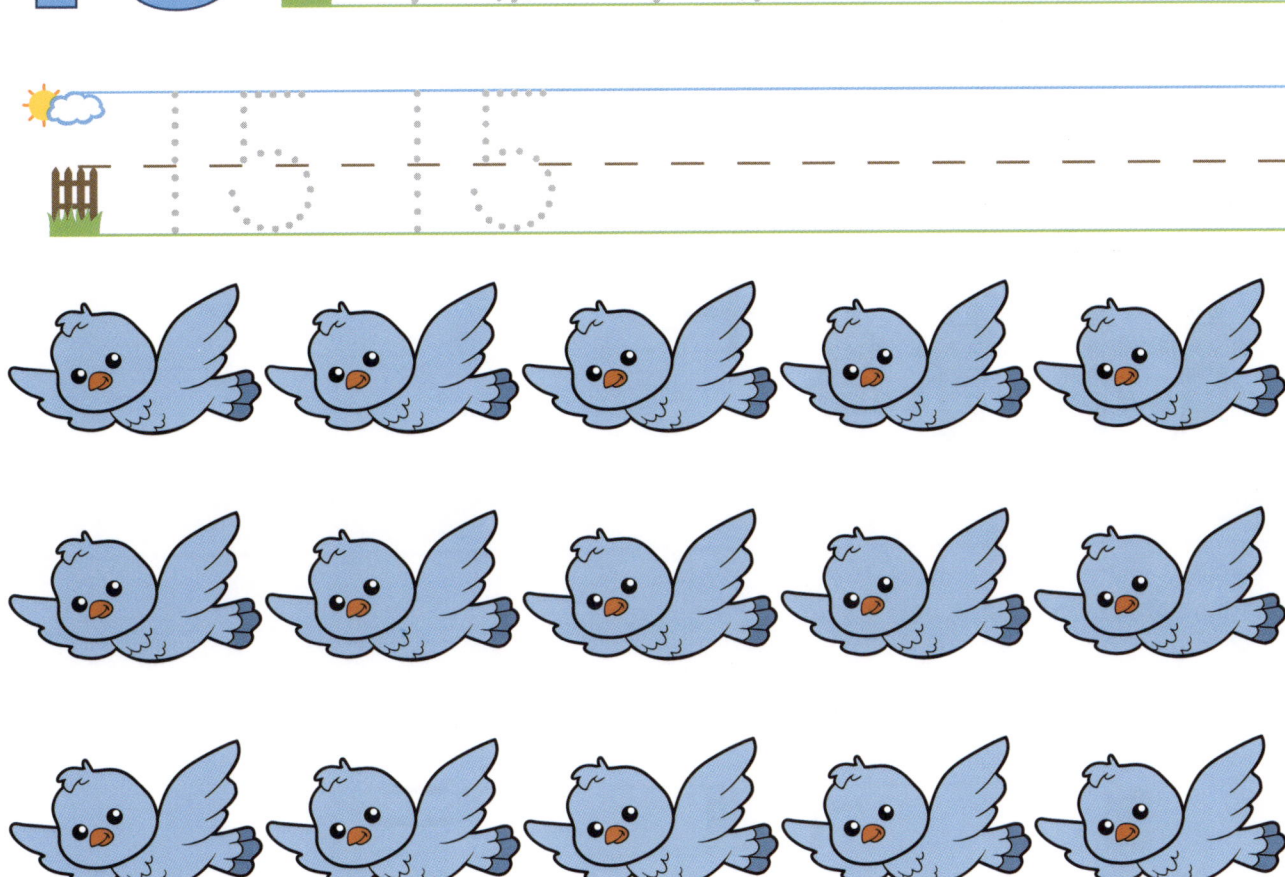

Count on...

12 13 14 ___

Directions: Skywrite the number 15 five times in the air with an invisible pencil. Trace the number 15, and write it on your own. Count the birds. Then, count on by ones to fill in the missing number.

DAY 109

Name: _____

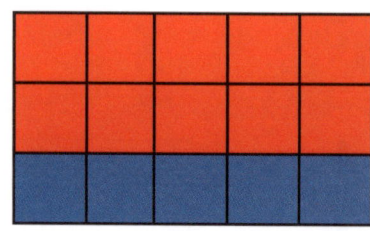

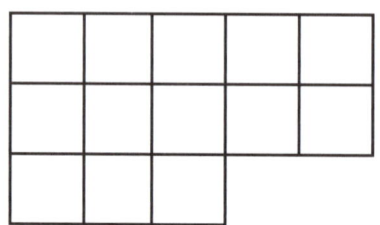

10 and 5 make 15 | 10 and 3 make 13

Directions: Count the objects or dots in each row. Write how many in all in each box. Color the pictures. Then, use two different colors to represent each number as you make the new numbers.

Add & Compose Numbers to 15

Name: _____

DAY 110

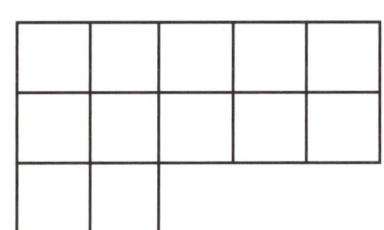

10 and 2 make 12

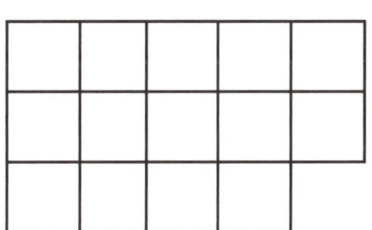

10 and 4 make 14

Directions: Count the objects or dots in each row. Write how many in all in each box. Color the pictures. Then, use two different colors to represent each number as you make the new numbers.

Add & Compose Numbers to 15

DAY 111

Name: _____

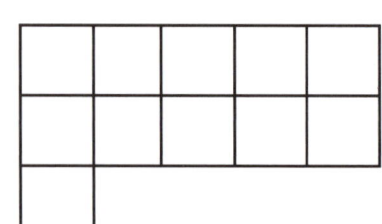

10 and 1 make 11

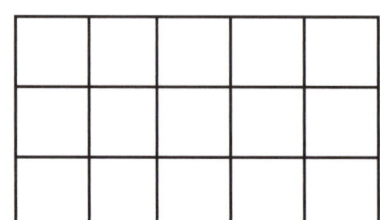

10 and 5 make 15

Directions: Count the objects or dots in each row. Write how many in all in each box. Color the pictures. Then, use two different colors to represent each number as you make the new numbers.

Name: _____

DAY 112

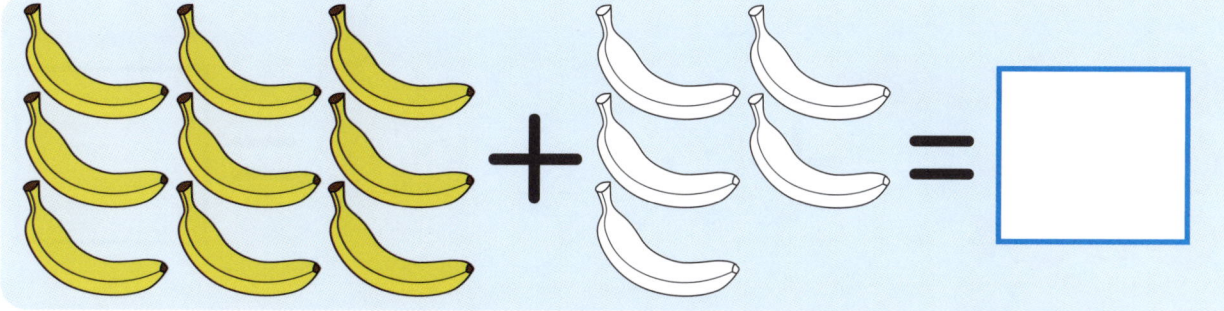

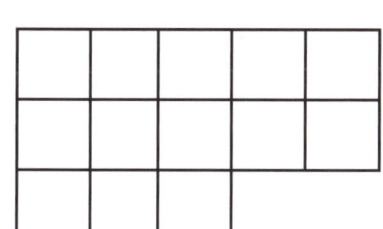

10 and 3 make 13

10 and 4 make 14

Add & Compose Numbers to 15

Directions: Count the objects or dots in each row. Write how many in all in each box. Color the pictures. Then, use two different colors to represent each number as you make the new numbers.

Name: _____

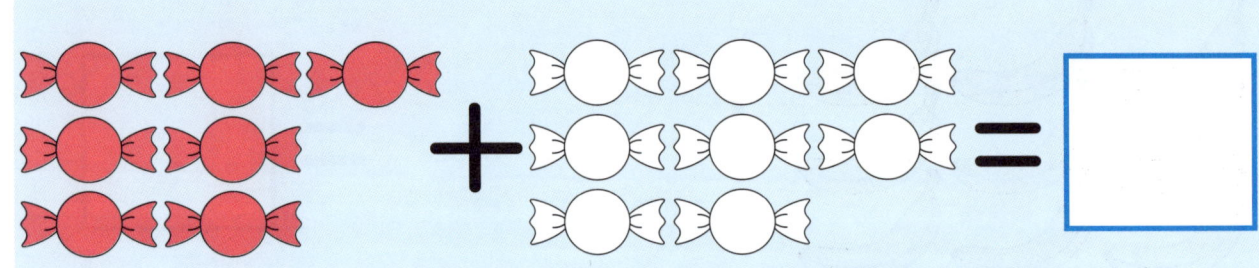

10 and 5 make 15

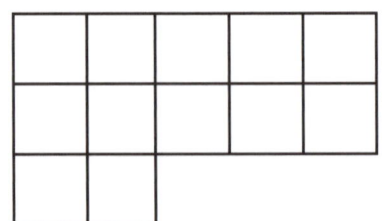

10 and 2 make 12

Directions: Count the objects or dots in each row. Write how many in all in each box. Color the pictures. Then, use two different colors to represent each number as you make the new numbers.

Name: _____

DAY 114

15 − 7 = ☐

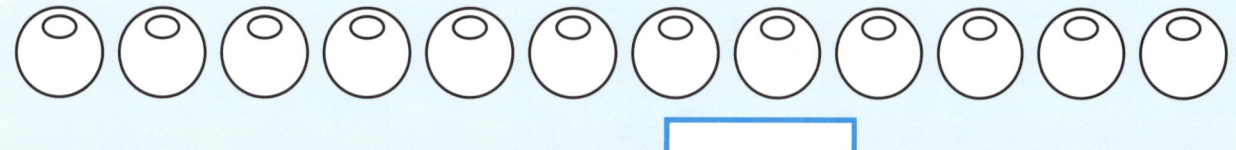

12 − 9 = ☐

This is one way to decompose 15:

15 made with 8 and 7

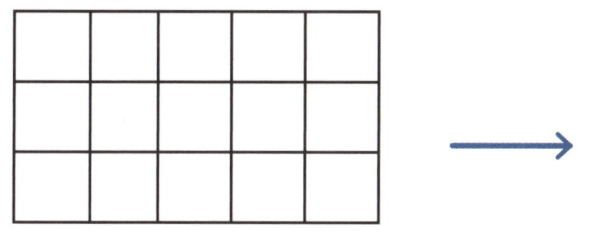 

15 made with 10 and 5

Directions: Count the objects in each section. Mark an *X* on the objects taken away. Color the objects that are left over. Write the amount in each box. Then, use two different colors to show how you decomposed the number.

Subtract & Decompose Numbers to 15

Name: _____

13 − 7 = ☐

14 − 5 = ☐

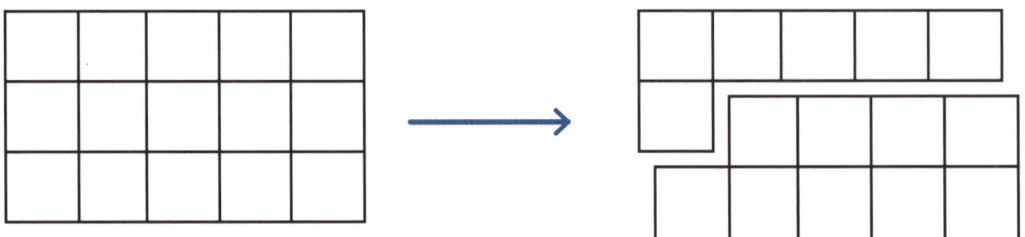

15 made with 6 and 9

Directions: Count the objects in each section. Mark an X on the objects taken away. Color the objects that are left over. Write the amount in each box. Then, use two different colors to show how you decomposed the number.

Name: _____

DAY 116

$15 - 5 =$ ☐

$13 - 9 =$ ☐

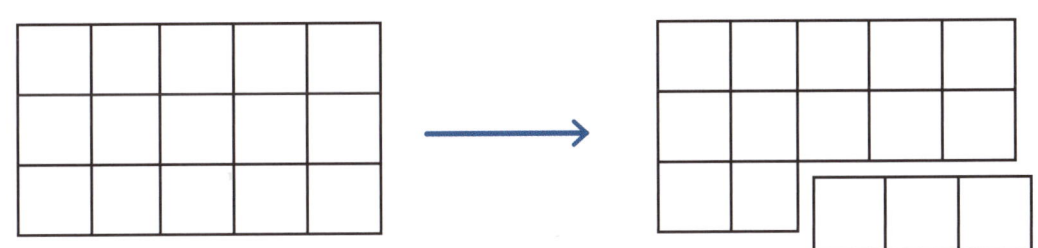

15 made with 12 and 3

Directions: Count the objects in each section. Mark an X on the objects taken away. Color the objects that are left over. Write the amount in each box. Then, use two different colors to show how you decomposed the number.

Name: _____

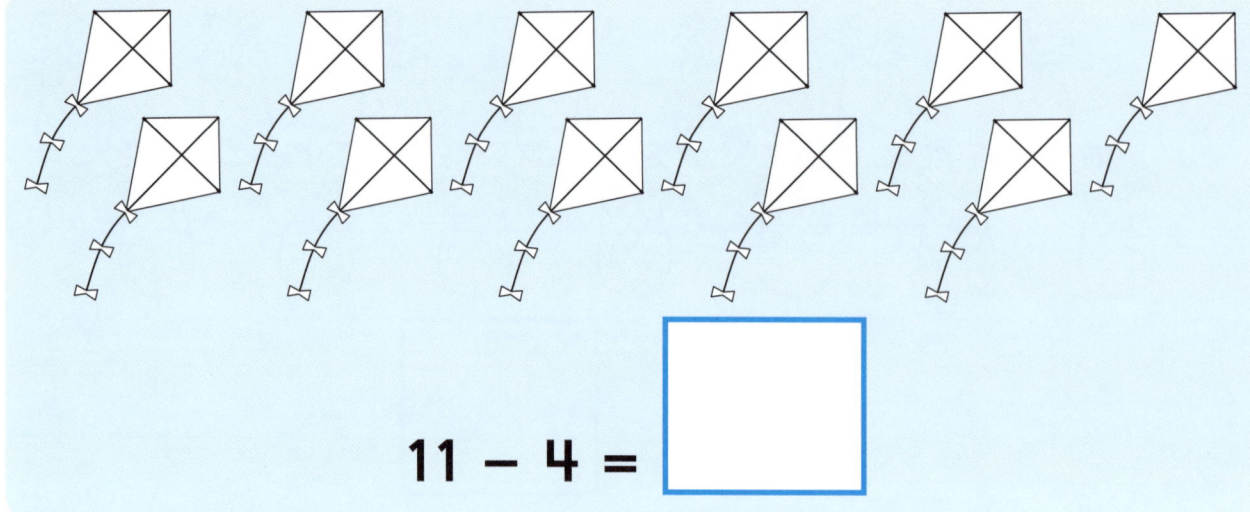

11 − 4 = ☐

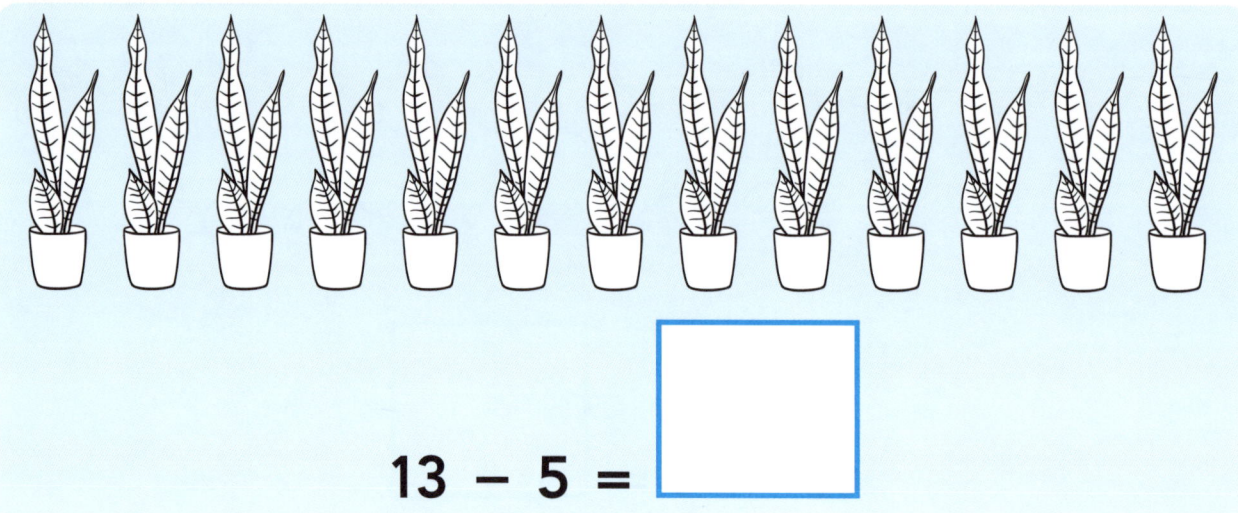

13 − 5 = ☐

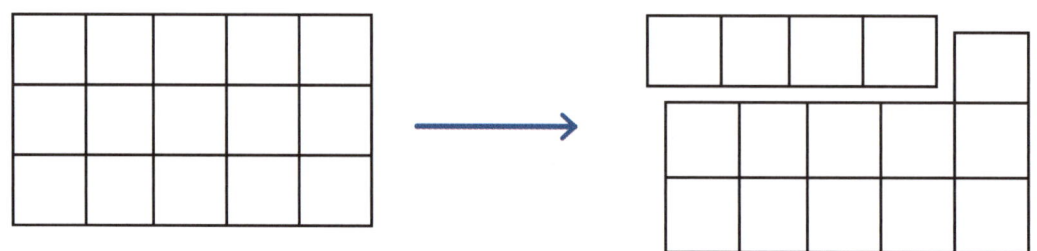

15 made with 4 and 11

Directions: Count the objects in each section. Mark an X on the objects taken away. Color the objects that are left over. Write the amount in each box. Then, use two different colors to show how you decomposed the number.

Name: _____

12 − 8 = ☐

15 − 5 = ☐

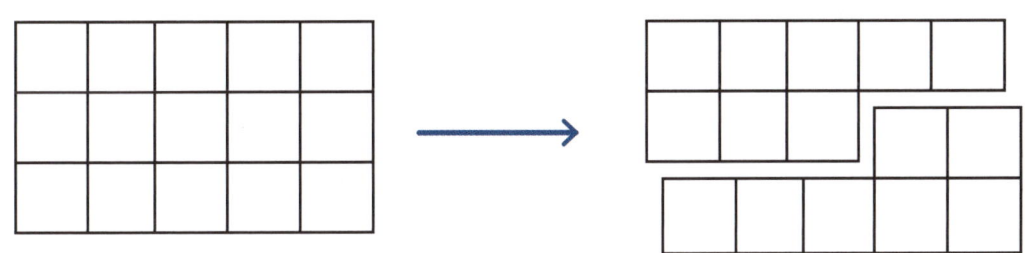

15 made with 8 and 7

Directions: Count the objects in each section. Mark an X on the objects taken away. Color the objects that are left over. Write the amount in each box. Then, use two different colors to show how you decomposed the number.

DAY 119

Name: _____

12 > 7   15 = 15   6 < 14

Remember that a shark ALWAYS wants to eat the bigger number!

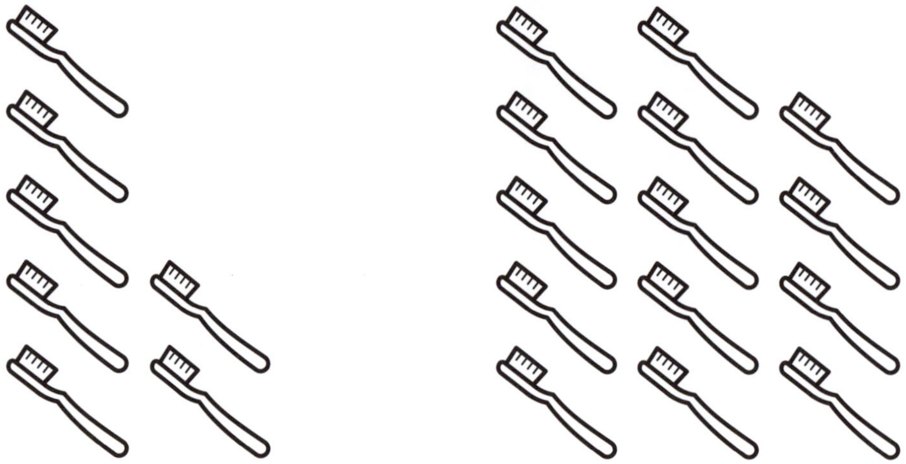

Compare Numbers Up to 15

7   > = <   14

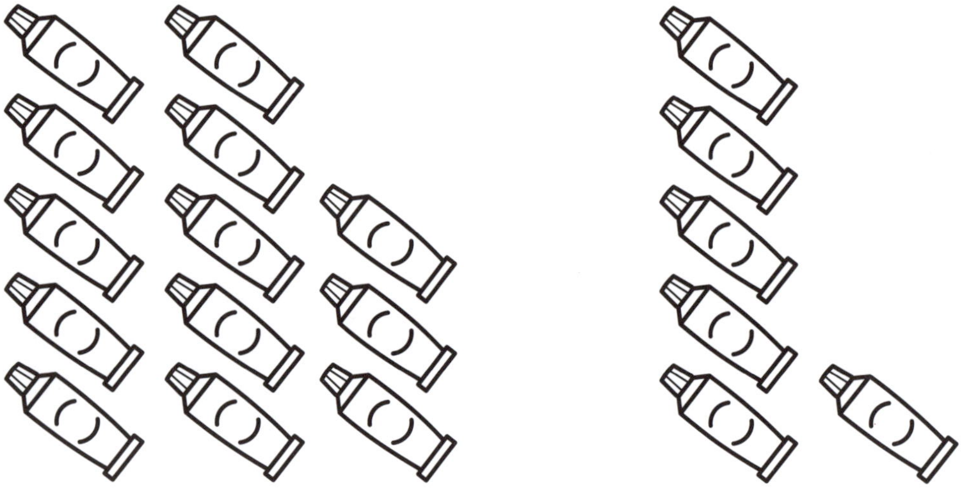

13   > = <   6

Directions: Count the objects in each section. Compare the two numbers in each section. Circle one of these signs > = <. Color the pictures.

Name: ______________________

14

12

14 = 14

13

15

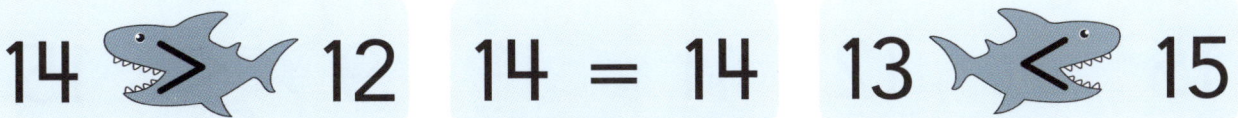

Remember that a shark ALWAYS wants to eat the bigger number!

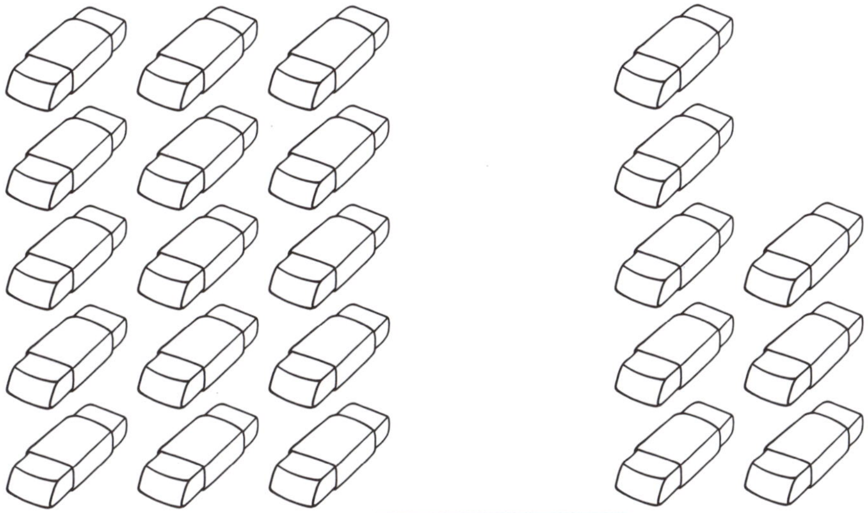

15 > = < 8

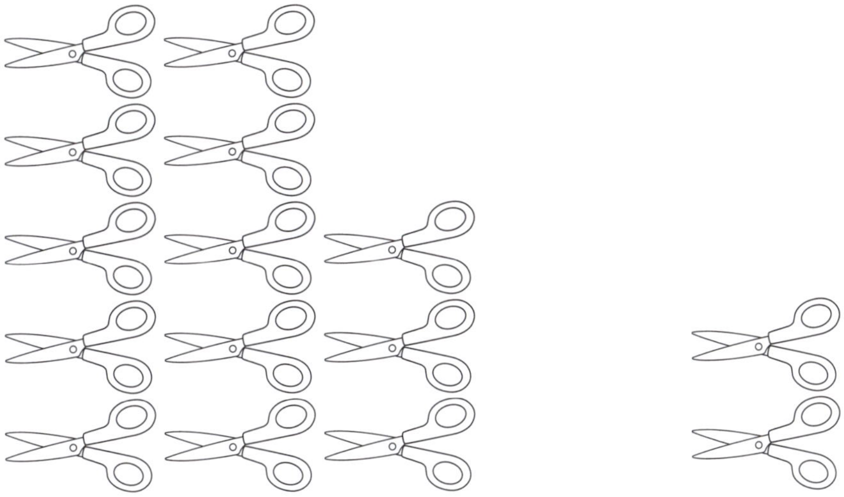

13 > = < 2

Directions: Count the objects in each section. Compare the two numbers in each section. Circle one of these signs > = <. Color the pictures.

DAY 121

Name: _____

15 🦈 12   11 = 11   9 🦈 15

Remember that a shark ALWAYS wants to eat the bigger number!

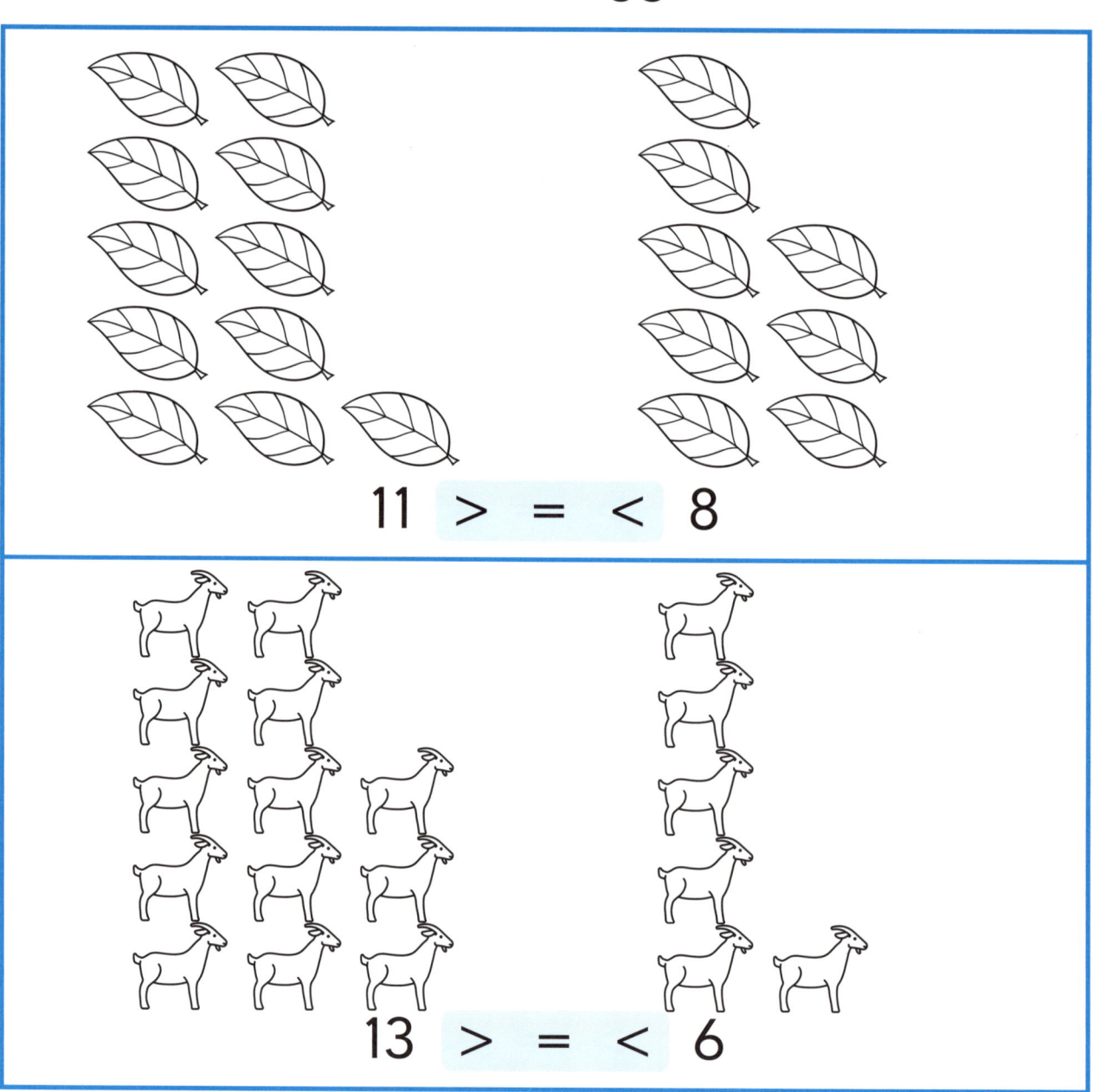

11   > = <   8

13   > = <   6

Directions: Count the objects in each section. Compare the two numbers in each section. Circle one of these signs > = <. Color the pictures.

Name: _____

DAY 122

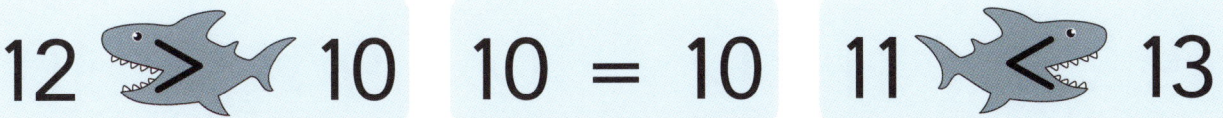

Remember that a shark ALWAYS wants to eat the bigger number!

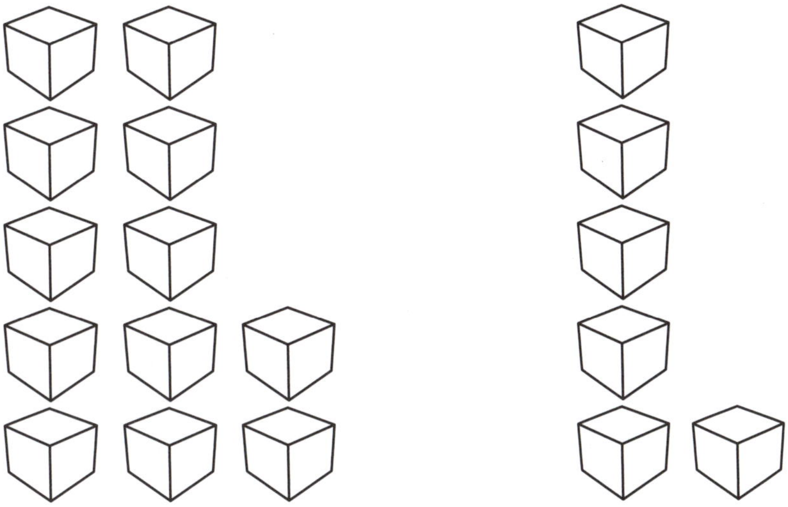

12   > = <   6

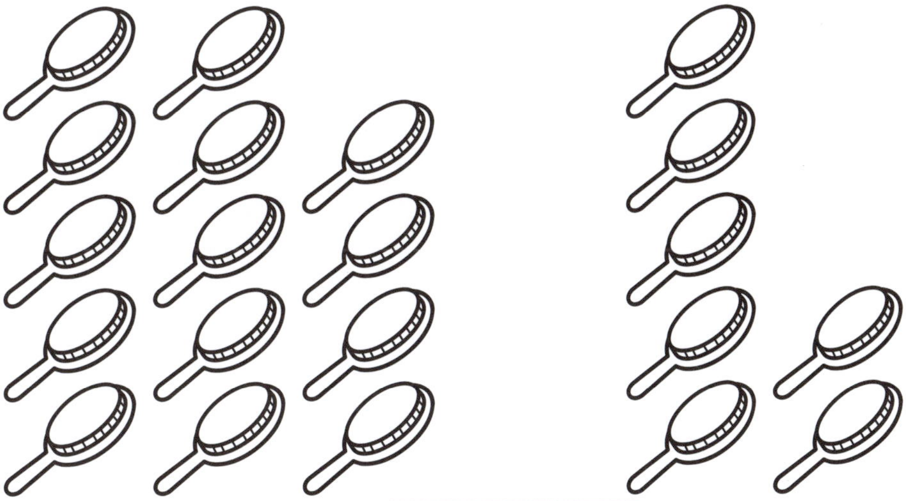

14   > = <   7

Directions: Count the objects in each section. Compare the two numbers in each section. Circle one of these signs > = <. Color the pictures.

Compare Numbers Up to 15

DAY 123

Name: _____

14 > 11   12 = 12   9 < 10

Remember that a shark ALWAYS wants to eat the bigger number!

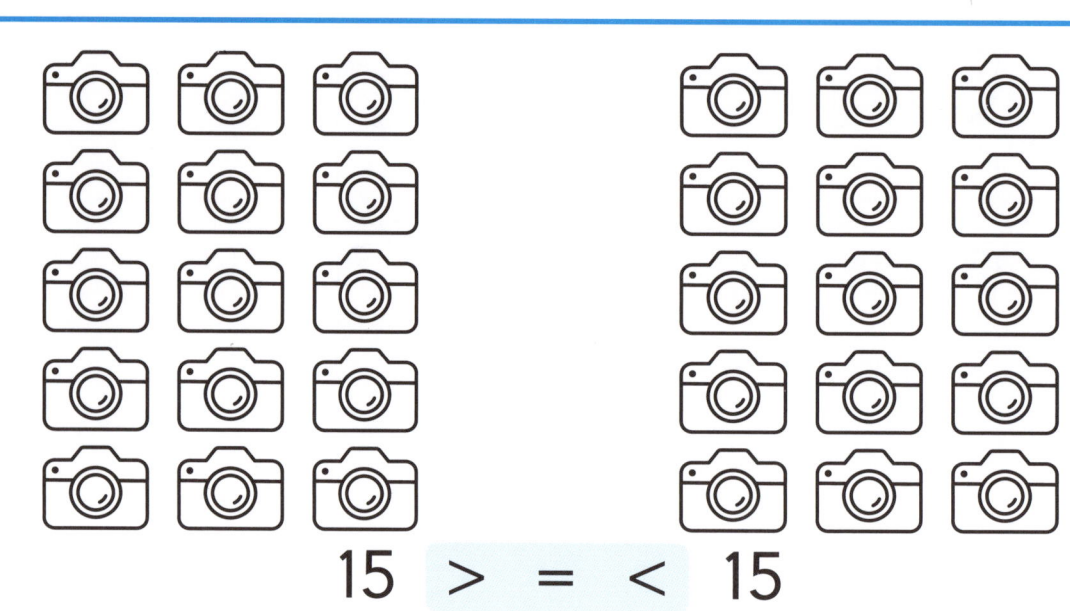

15   > = <   15

2   > = <   12

Directions: Count the objects in each section. Compare the two numbers in each section. Circle one of these signs > = <. Color the pictures.

Name: _____

DAY 124

Name Numbers 16–20

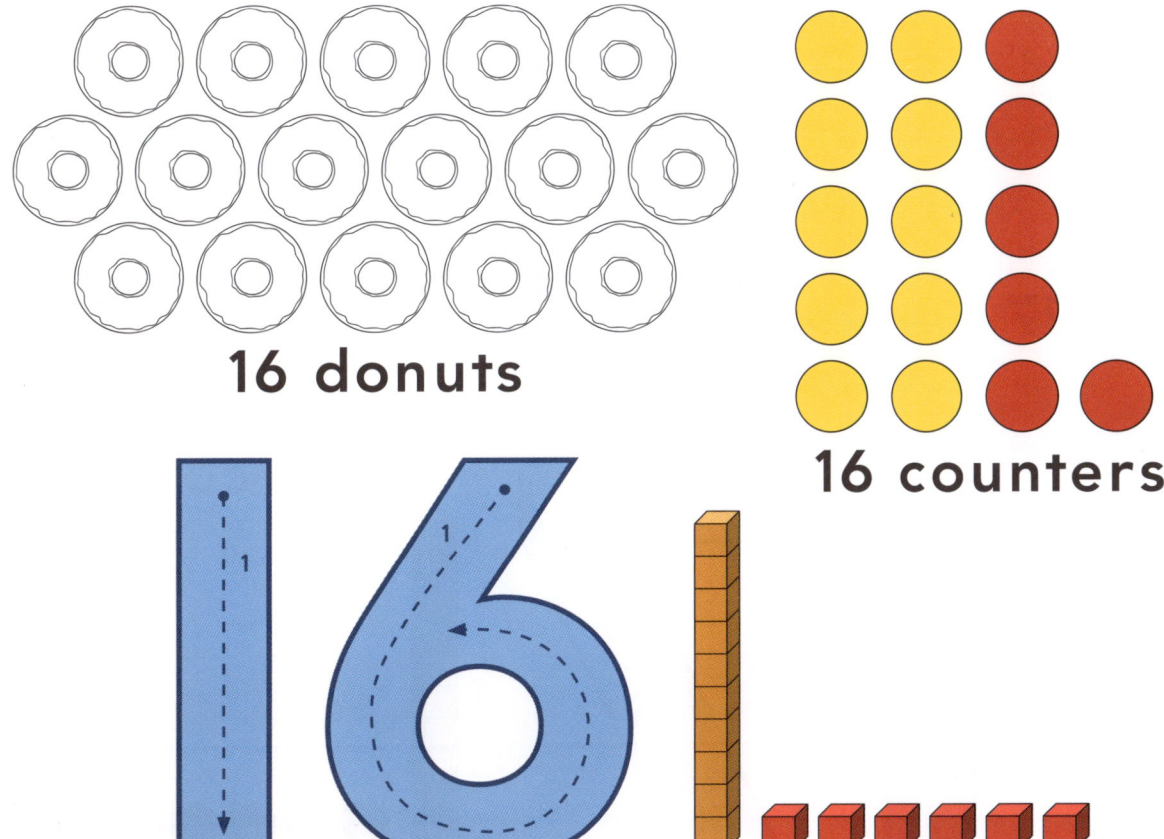

16 donuts

16 counters

16
sixteen

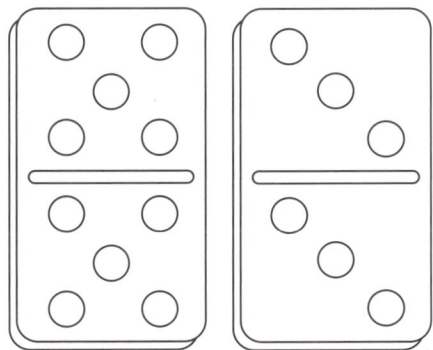

16 dots

Time to Draw

Directions: Trace the 16 at least 10 times with your finger. Say its name as you do this. Count the objects in each picture. Color the pictures. Circle each number 16. Then, draw 16 objects, shapes, or letters.

DAY 125

Name: _____

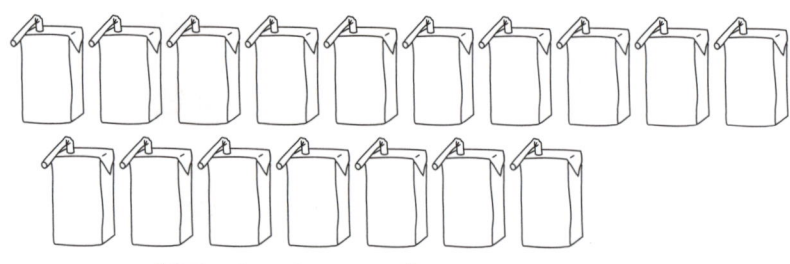
17 juice boxes

17 counters

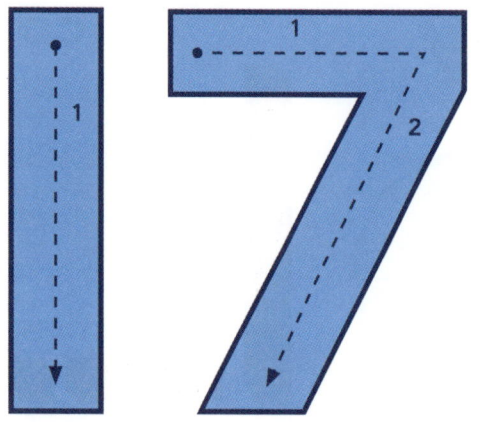
seventeen

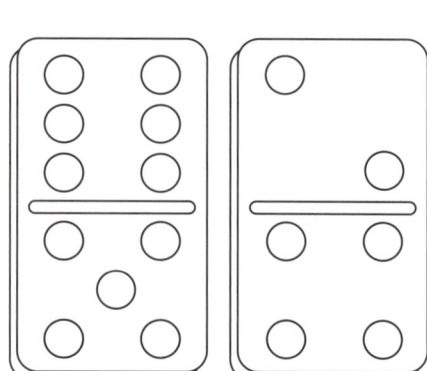
17 dots

Name Numbers 16–20

Time to Draw

Directions: Trace the 17 at least 10 times with your finger. Say its name as you do this. Count the objects in each picture. Color the pictures. Circle each number 17. Then, draw 17 objects, shapes, or letters.

142   127443—180 Days of Math   © Shell Education

Name: _____

18 apples

eighteen

18 counters

18 dots

Directions: Trace the 18 at least 10 times with your finger. Say its name as you do this. Count the objects in each picture. Color the pictures. Circle each number 18. Then, go on a scavenger hunt to look for 18 objects. Draw what you find.

DAY 126

Name Numbers 16–20

Time to Draw

DAY 127

Name: _____

19 grapes

19 counters

nineteen

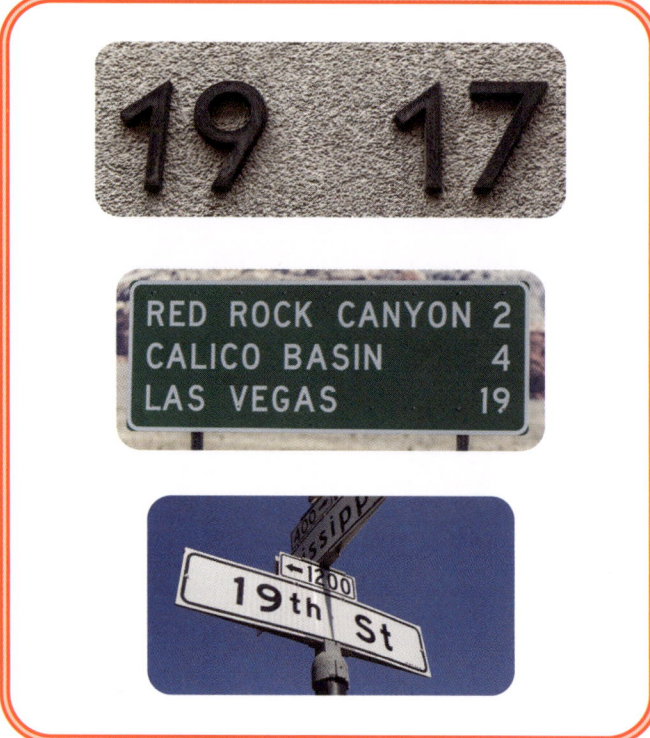

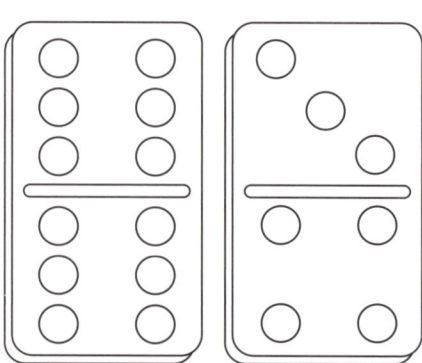
19 dots

Directions: Trace the 19 at least 10 times with your finger. Say its name as you do this. Count the objects in each picture. Color the pictures. Circle each number 19. Then, find and put a box around the number 19 in the images.

Name: _____

DAY 128

20 dogs

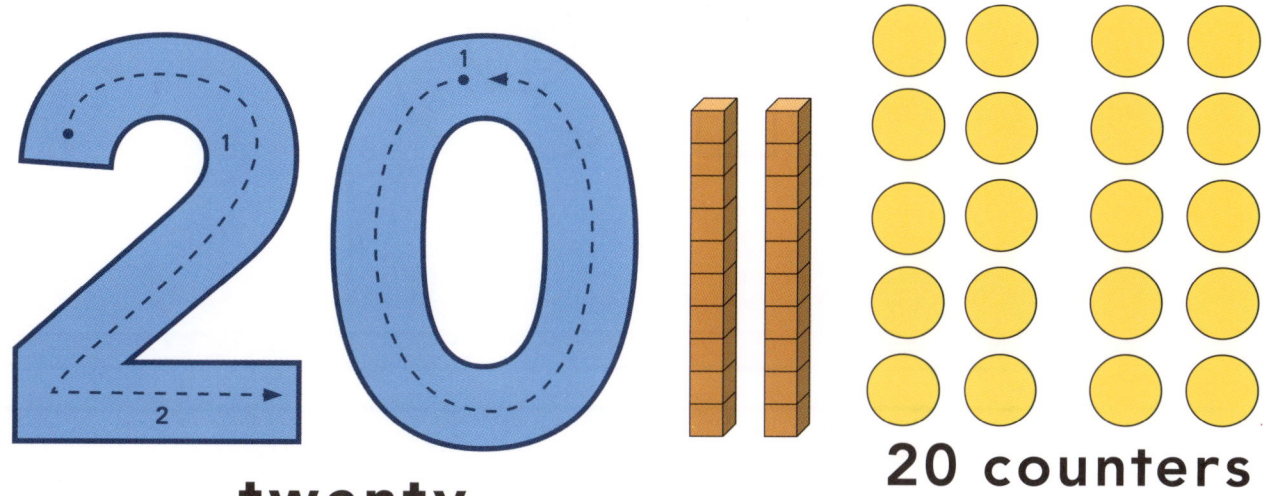

twenty   20 counters

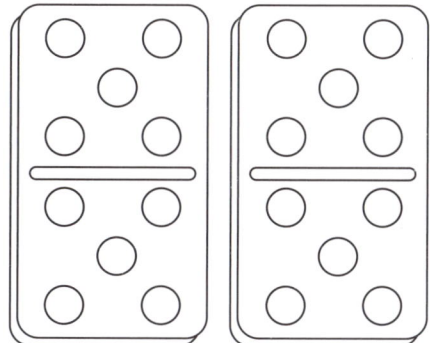

20 dots

Time to Draw

Directions: Trace the 20 at least 10 times with your finger. Say its name as you do this. Count the objects in each picture. Color the pictures. Circle each number 20. Then, draw 20 objects, shapes, or letters.

Name Numbers 16–20

© Shell Education   127443—180 Days of Math   145

DAY 129

Name: _____

Count by Ones to 20

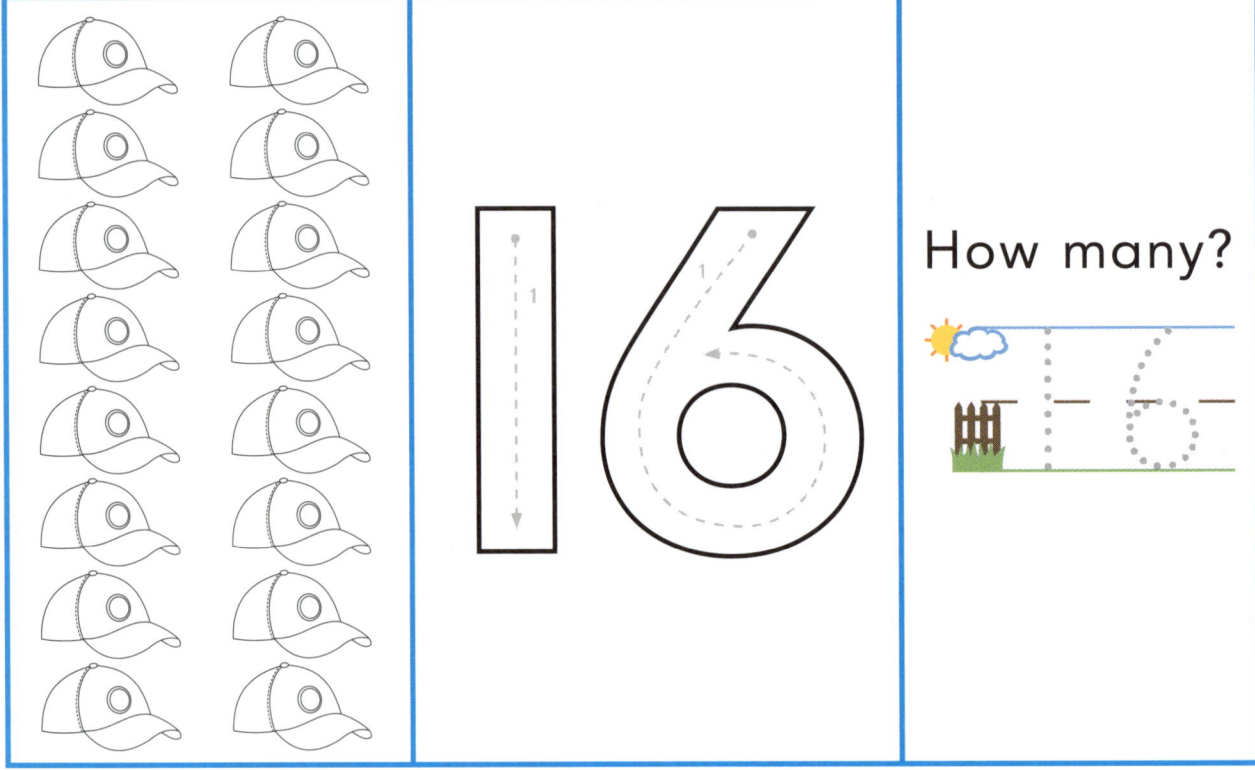

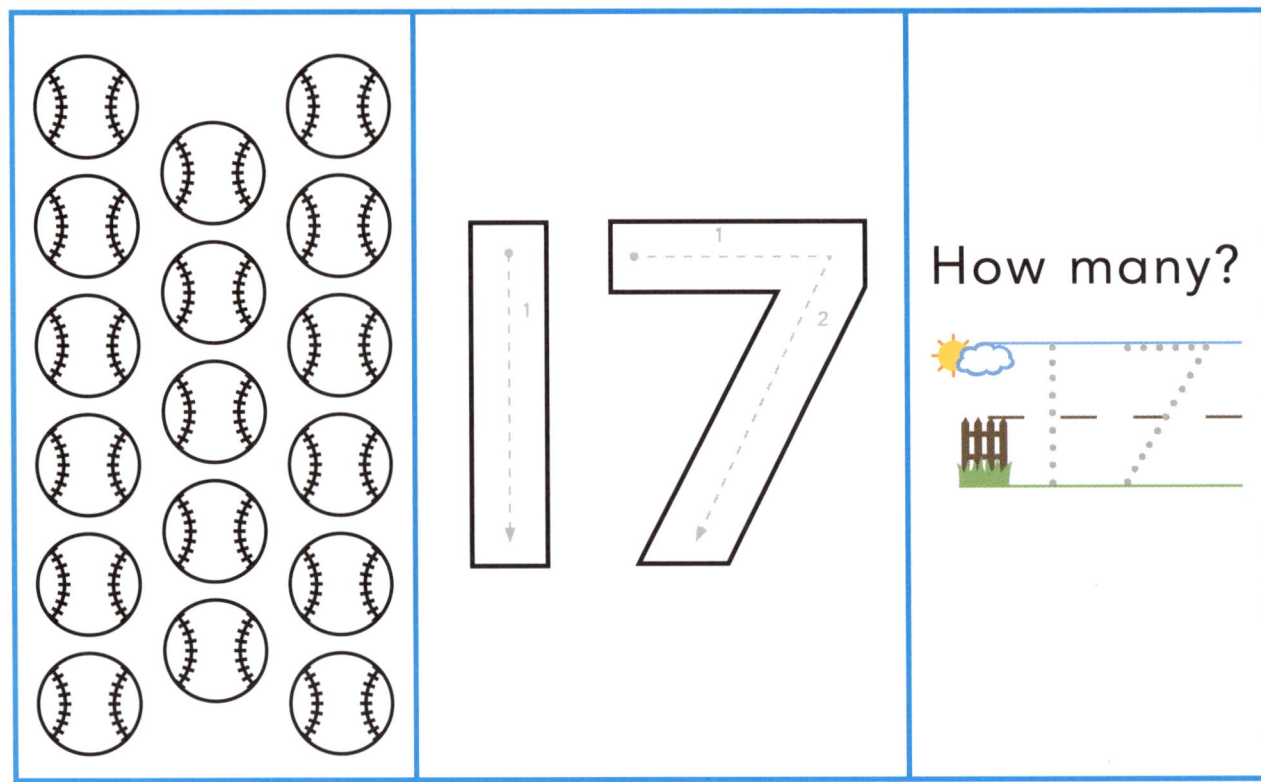

Directions: Count the objects in each row. Write the number of objects in each row. Color the pictures and numbers.

Name: _____

DAY 130

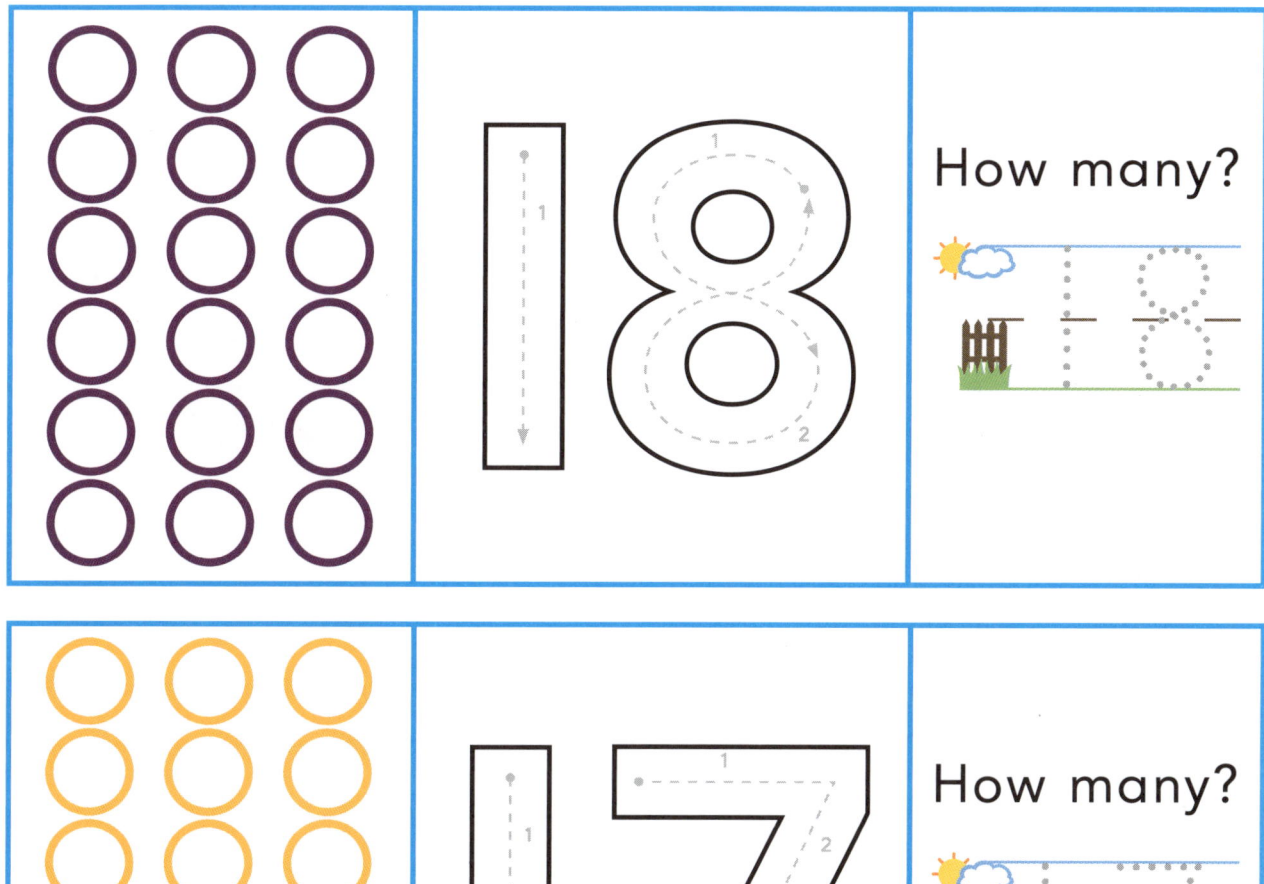

How many? 18

How many? 17

Count by Ones to 20

Which number is less: 18 or 17?

_____

Directions: Place one small object in each purple circle. Count the objects in the purple circles. Write the number of objects on the line. Color the purple circles. Do the same steps for the yellow circles. Then, answer the question.

DAY 131

Name: _____

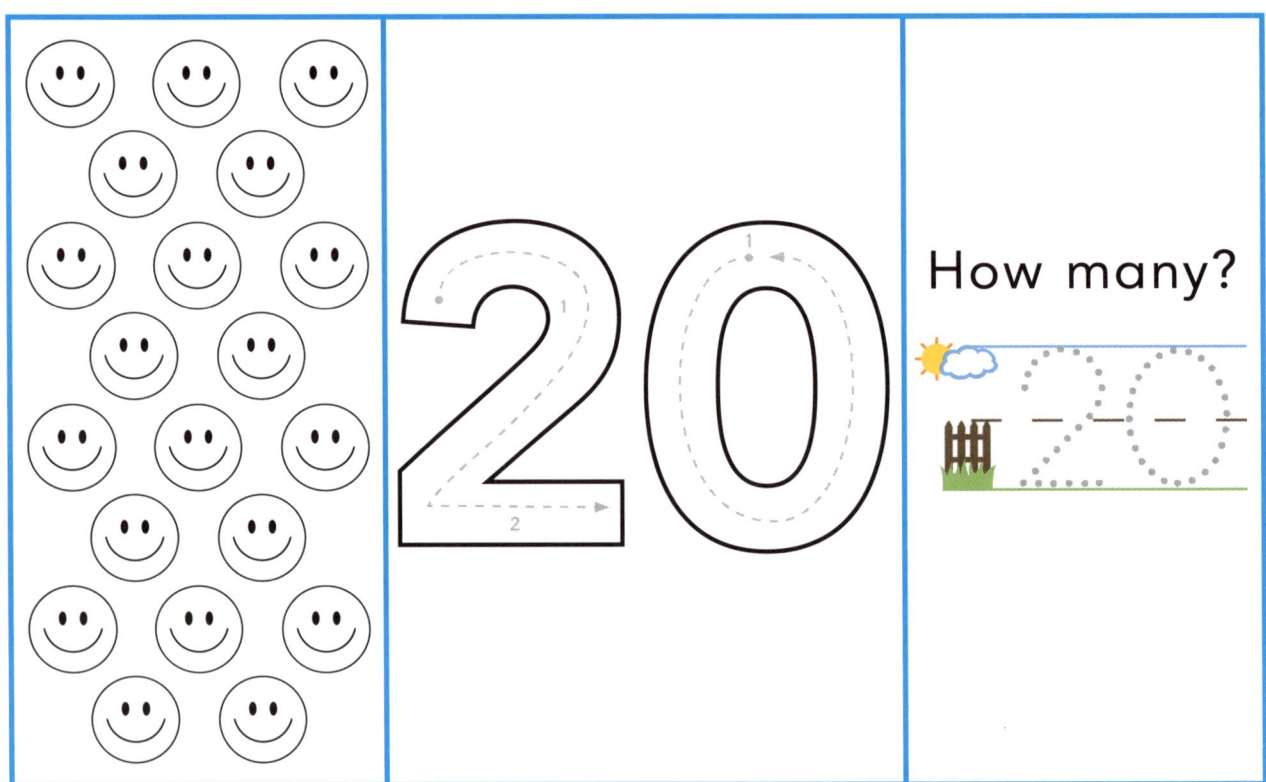

Count by Ones to 20

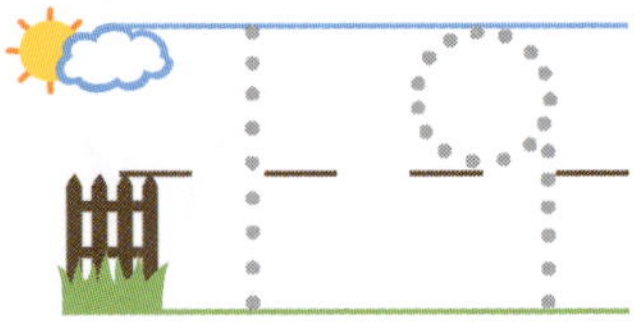

Directions: Count the objects in each row. Write the number of objects in each row. Color the pictures and numbers.

Name: _____

DAY 132

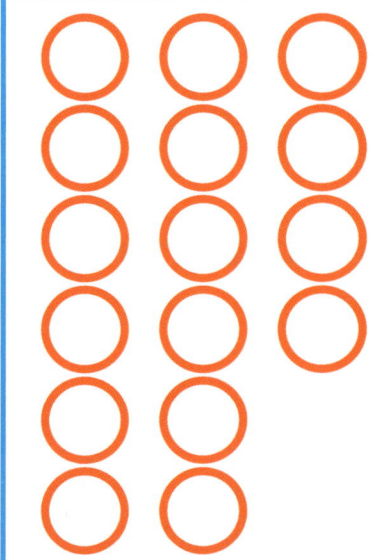 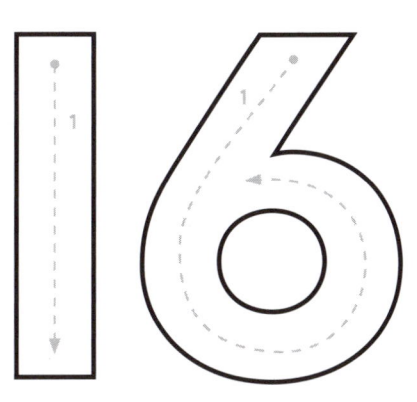 How many?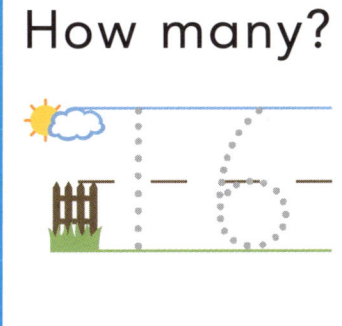

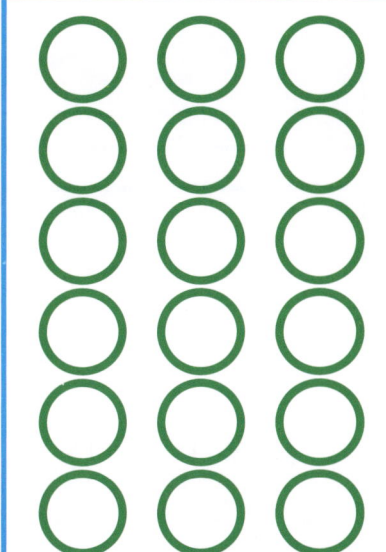  How many?

Count by Ones to 20

Which number is less: 16 or 18?

Directions: Place one small object in each orange circle. Count the objects in the orange circles. Write the number of objects on the line. Color the orange circles. Do the same steps for the green circles. Then, answer the question.

DAY 133

Name: _____

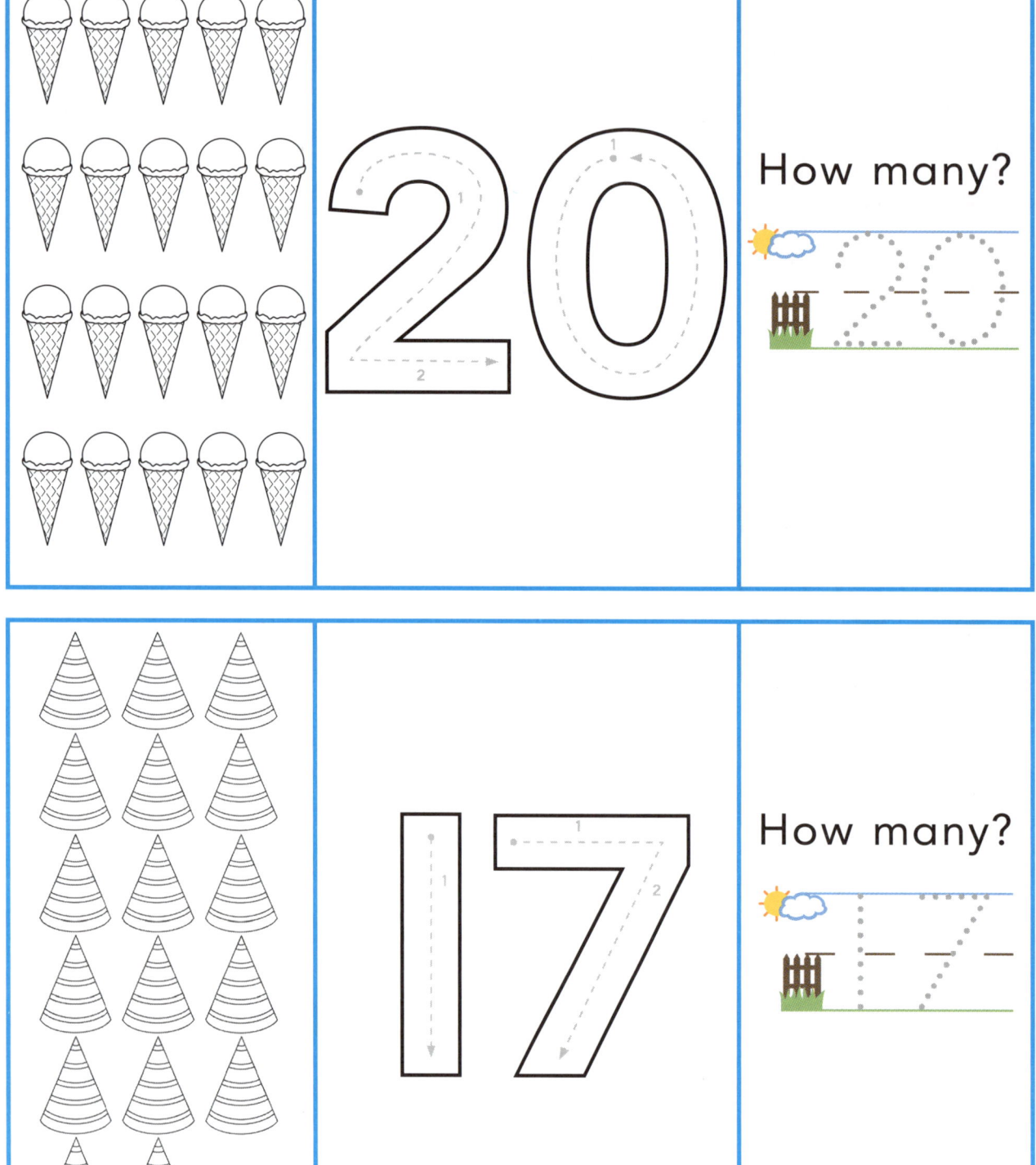

Directions: Count the objects in each row. Write the number of objects in each row. Color the pictures and numbers.

Name: _____

DAY 134

16	20	19	20	18
20	18	20	16	17
18	16	17	19	19
17	19	18	18	20
19	17	16	17	16

Identify Numbers 16–20

How many 16s did you find?

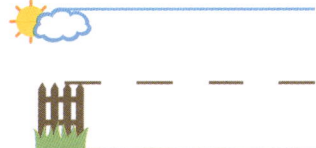

Directions: Find every number 16, and color those squares pink. Answer the question. Then, make the number 16 with clay or small objects.

DAY 135

Name: _____

Directions: Find and circle every number 17. Color the drawings of the number 17. Then, skywrite the number 17 at least five times in the air using an invisible pencil. Hop 17 times.

DAY 136

Name: _____

18	4	7	17	5
1	6	12	18	18
18	12	10	19	8
2	3	18	20	11
13	18	16	8	9

Identify Numbers 16–20

How many 18s did you find?

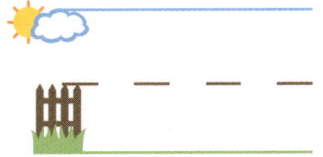

Directions: Find every number 18, and color those squares purple. Answer the question. Then, make the number 18 with clay or small objects.

DAY 137

Name: _____

Identify Numbers 16–20

Directions: Find and circle every number 19. Color the drawings of the number 19. Then, skywrite the number 19 at least five times in the air using an invisible pencil. Jump 19 times.

Name: _____

DAY 138

20	15	20	20	6
12	9	8	16	14
11	20	16	7	20
5	4	3	2	13
20	13	10	15	1

Identify Numbers 16–20

How many 20s did you find?

Directions: Find every number 20, and color those squares blue. Answer the question. Then, make the number 20 with clay or small objects.

DAY 139

Name: _____

Write Numbers from 16–20

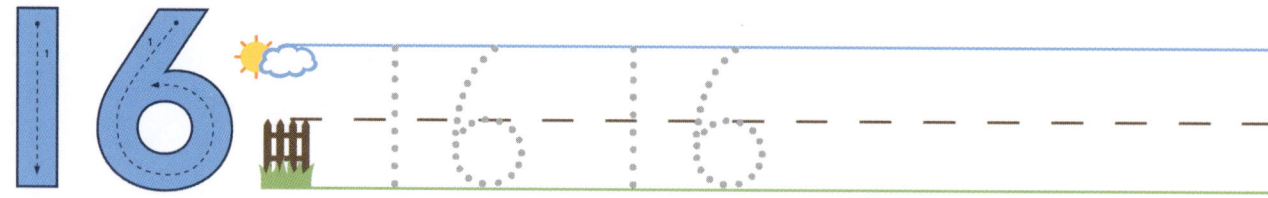

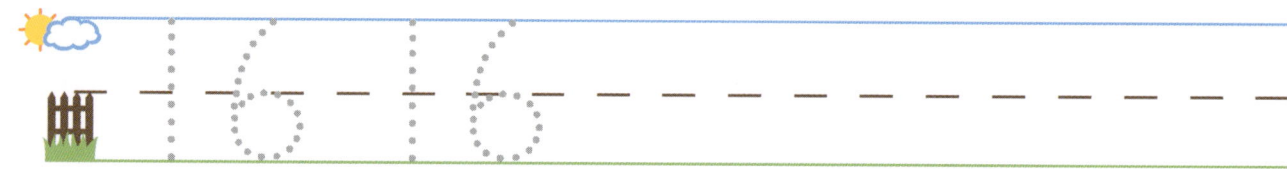

Count on...

Directions: Skywrite the number 16 five times in the air with an invisible pencil. Trace the number 16, and write it on your own. Count the butterflies. Then, count on by ones to fill in the missing number.

Name: _____

DAY 140

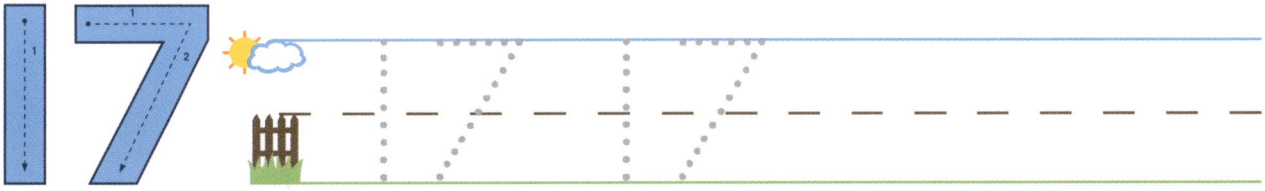

Count on...

Directions: Skywrite the number 17 five times in the air with an invisible pencil. Trace the number 17, and write it on your own. Count the horses. Then, count on by ones to fill in the missing number.

Write Numbers from 16–20

DAY 141

Name: _____

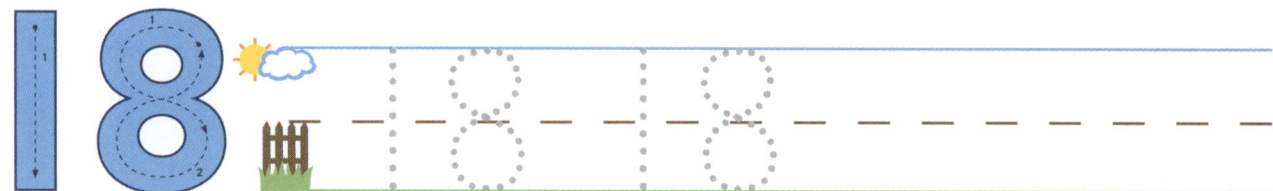

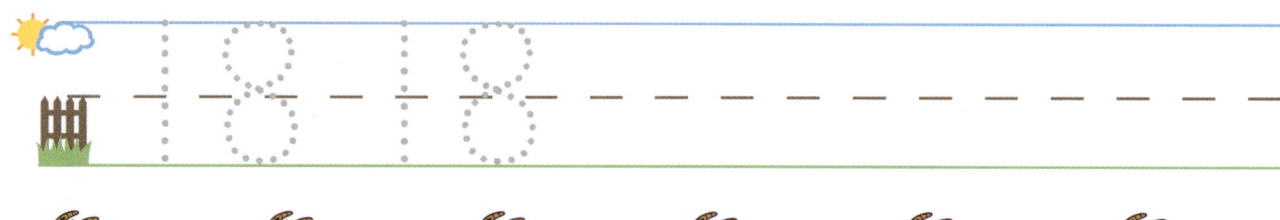

Count on...

Directions: Skywrite the number 18 five times in the air with an invisible pencil. Trace the number 18, and write it on your own. Count the goats. Then, count on by ones to fill in the missing number.

Name: _____

DAY 142

Write Numbers from 16–20

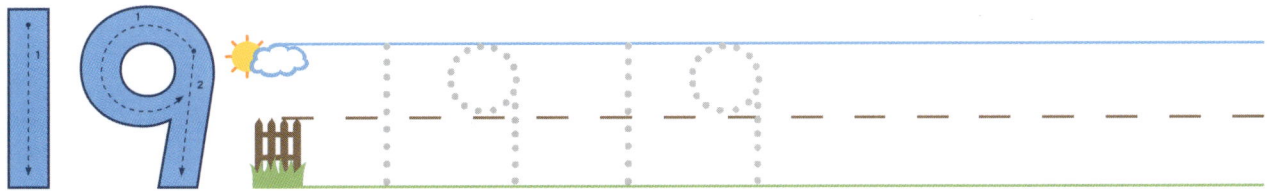

Count on...

Directions: Skywrite the number 19 five times in the air with an invisible pencil. Trace the number 19, and write it on your own. Count the sheep. Then, count on by ones to fill in the missing number.

DAY 143

Name: _____

20

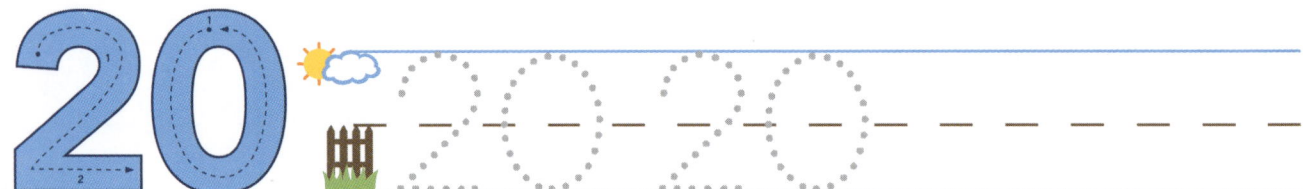

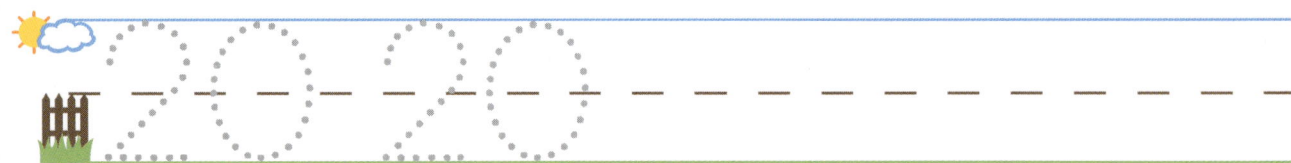

Count on...

Directions: Skywrite the number 20 five times in the air with an invisible pencil. Trace the number 20, and write it on your own. Count the cows. Then, count on by ones to fill in the missing number.

Name: _____

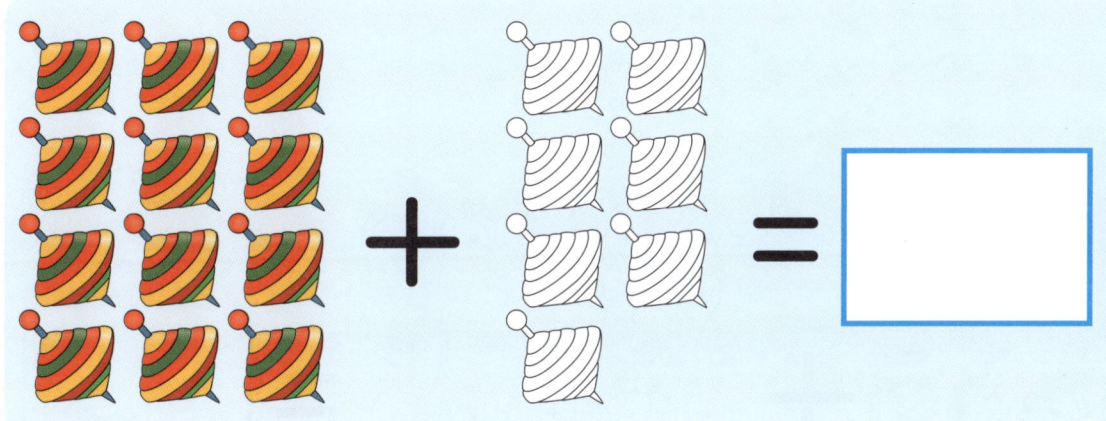

This is one way to compose 20:

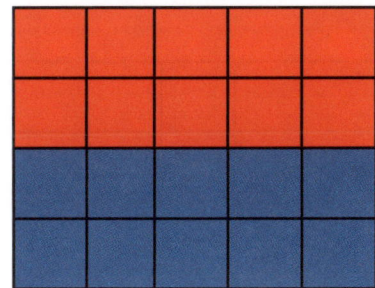

10 and 10 make 20

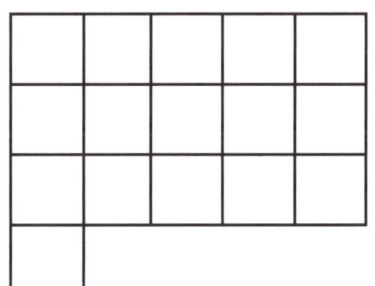

10 and 6 make 16

Directions: Count the objects in each row. Write how many in all in each box. Color the pictures. Then, use two different colors to represent each number as you make the new numbers.

DAY 145

Name: _____

10 and 8 make 18

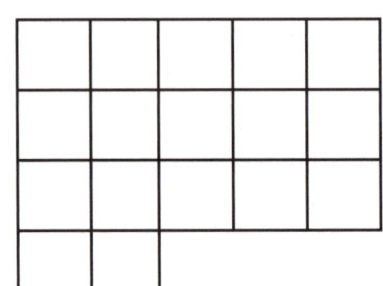

10 and 7 make 17

Directions: Count the objects in each row. Write how many in all in each box. Color the pictures. Then, use two different colors to represent each number as you make the new numbers.

Name: _____

DAY 146

10 and 9 make 19

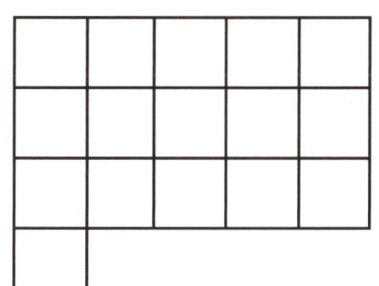
10 and 6 make 16

Add & Compose Numbers to 20

Directions: Count the objects in each row. Write how many in all in each box. Color the pictures. Then, use two different colors to represent each number as you make the new numbers.

DAY 147

Name: _____

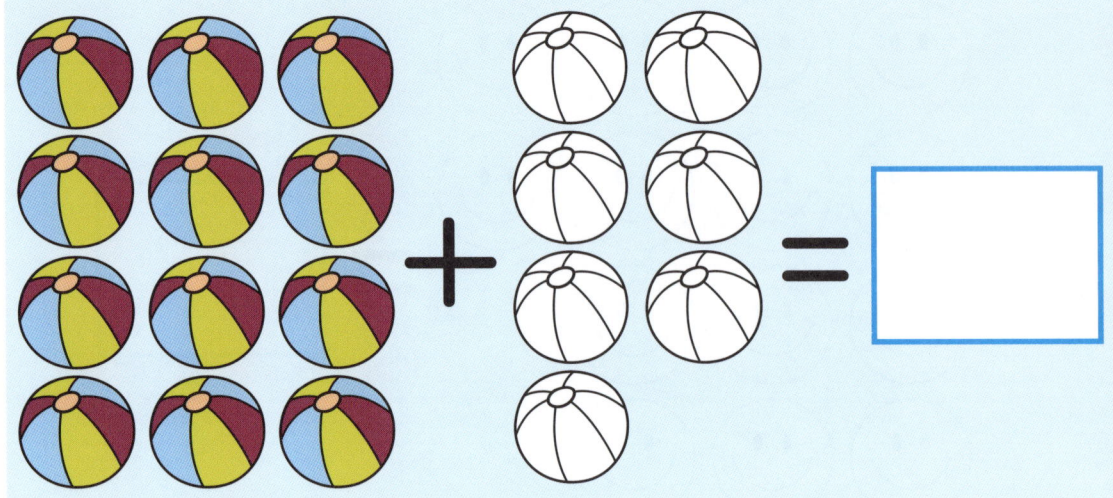

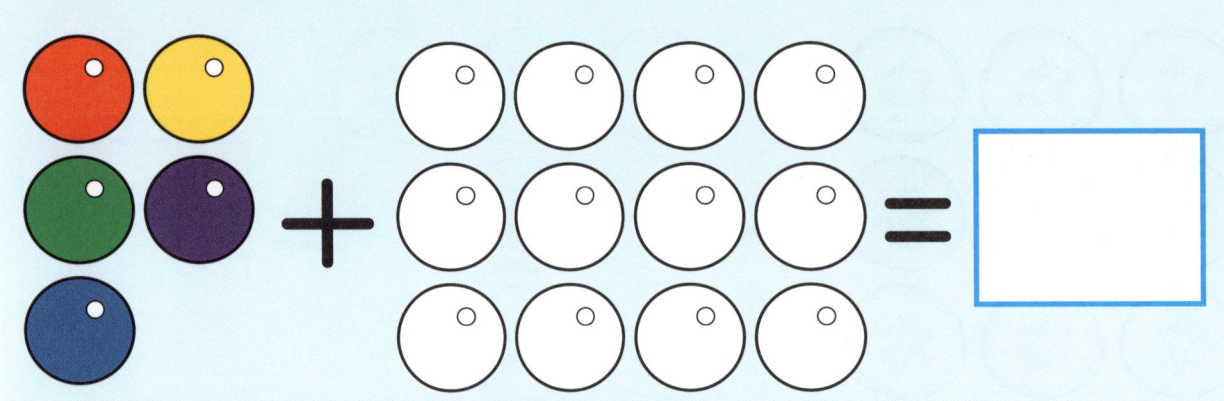

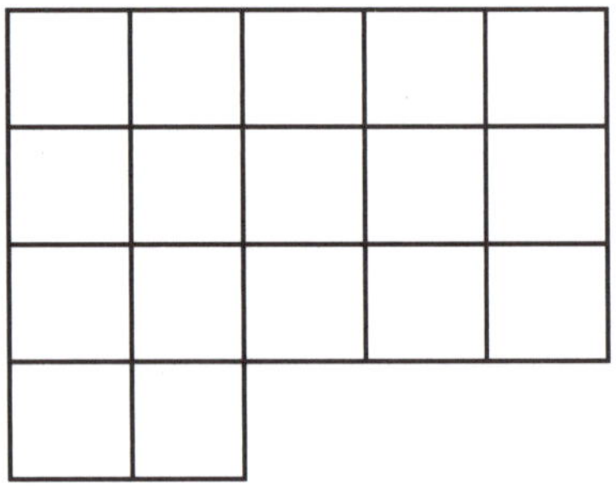

10 and 7 make 17 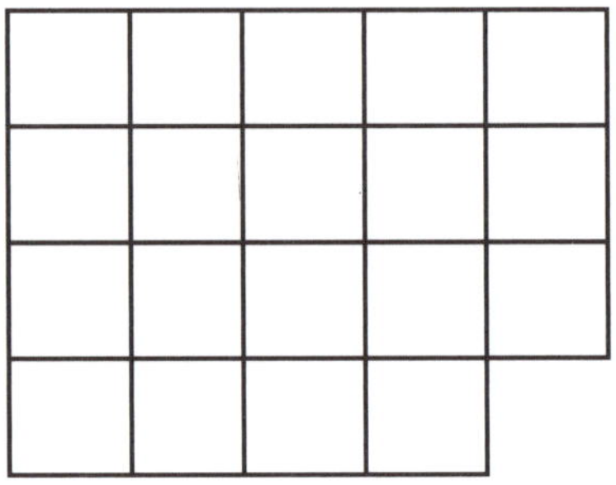 | 10 and 9 make 19

Directions: Count the objects in each row. Write how many in all in each box. Color the pictures. Then, use two different colors to represent each number as you make the new numbers.

Name: _____

DAY 148

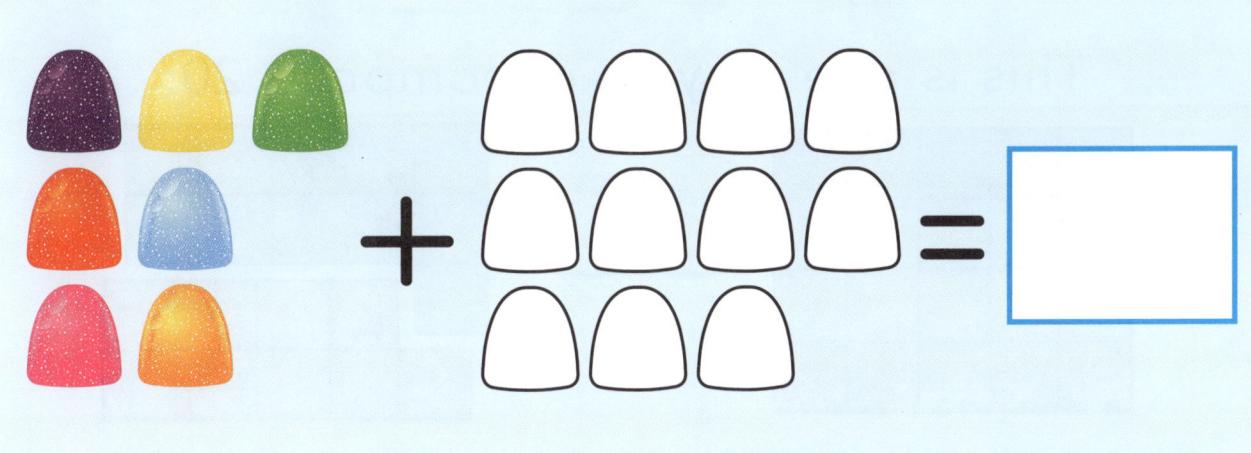

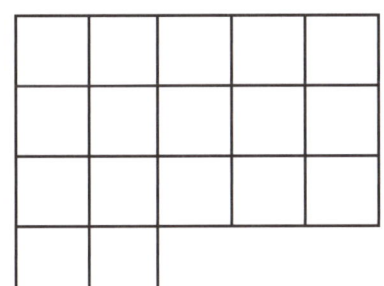

10 and 7 make 17

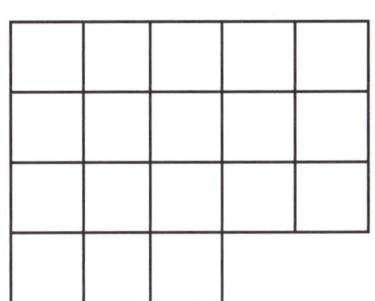

10 and 8 make 18

Directions: Count the objects in each row. Write how many in all in each box. Color the pictures. Then, use two different colors to represent each number as you make the new numbers.

Add & Compose Numbers to 20

DAY 149

Name: _____

16 − 7 = 9

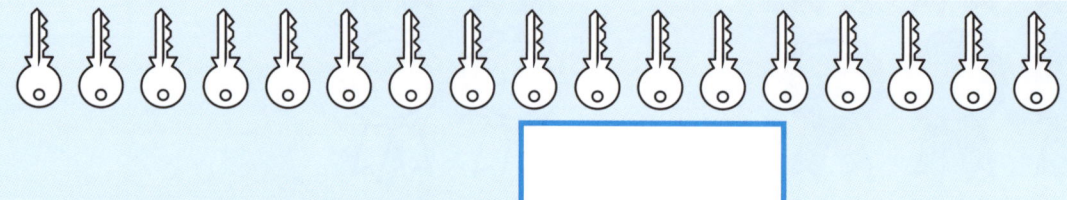

17 − 9 =

This is one way to decompose 20:

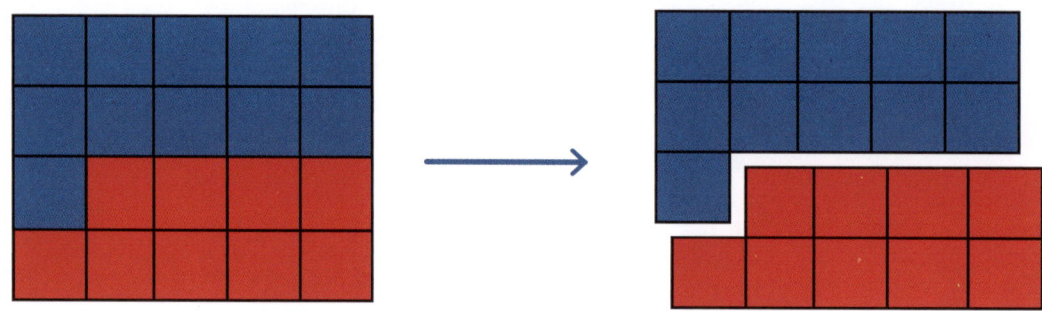

20 made with 11 and 9

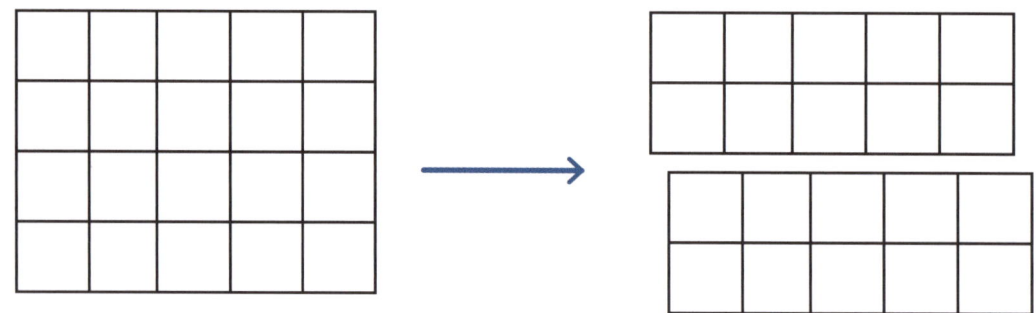

20 made with 10 and 10

Directions: Count the objects in each section. Mark an *X* on the objects taken away. Color the objects that are left over. Write the amount in each box. Then, use two different colors to show how you decomposed the number.

Name: _____

DAY 150

19 − 6 = ☐

16 − 5 = ☐

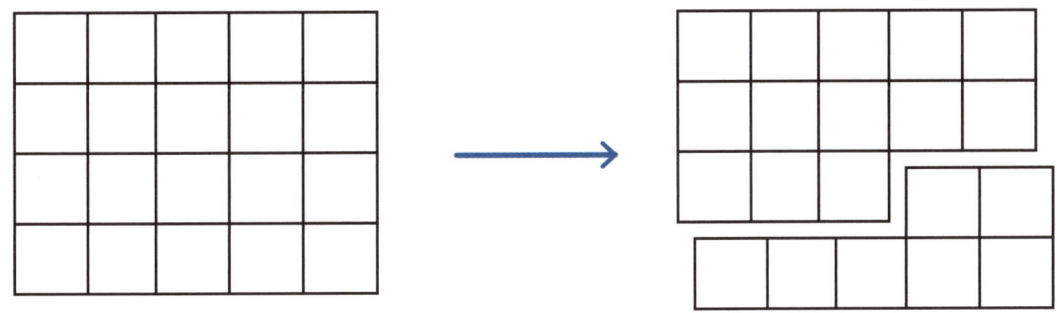

20 made with 13 and 7

Directions: Count the objects in each section. Mark an *X* on the objects taken away. Color the objects that are left over. Write the amount in each box. Then, use two different colors to show how you decomposed the number.

Subtract & Decompose Numbers to 20

DAY 151

Name: _____

19 − 7 = ☐

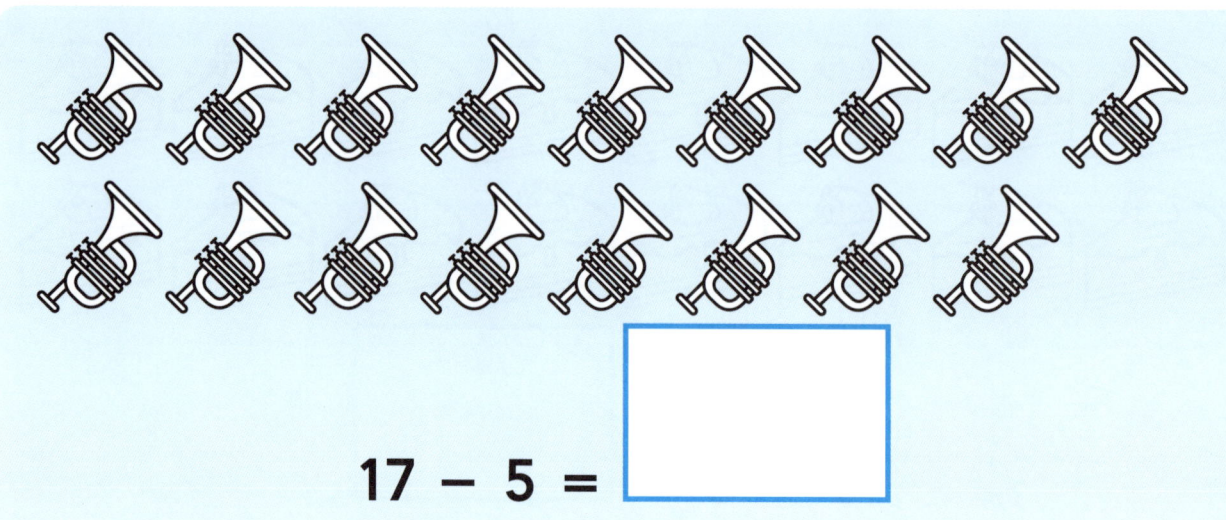

17 − 5 = ☐

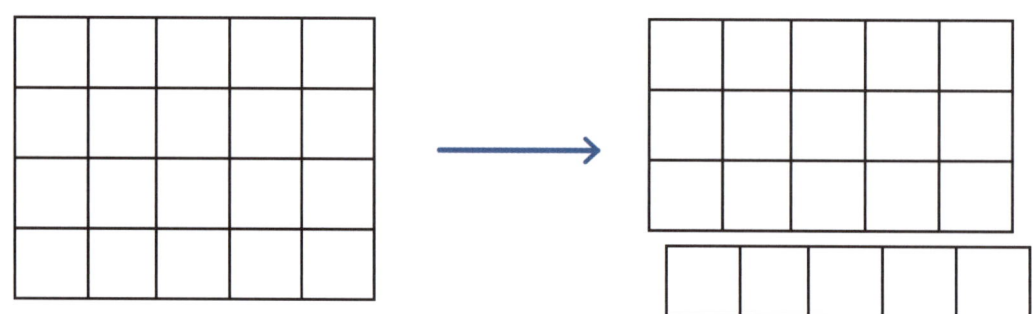

20 made with 15 and 5

Directions: Count the objects in each section. Mark an X on the objects taken away. Color the objects that are left over. Write the amount in each box. Then, use two different colors to show how you decomposed the number.

Name: _____

DAY 152

17 − 4 = ☐

16 − 11 = ☐

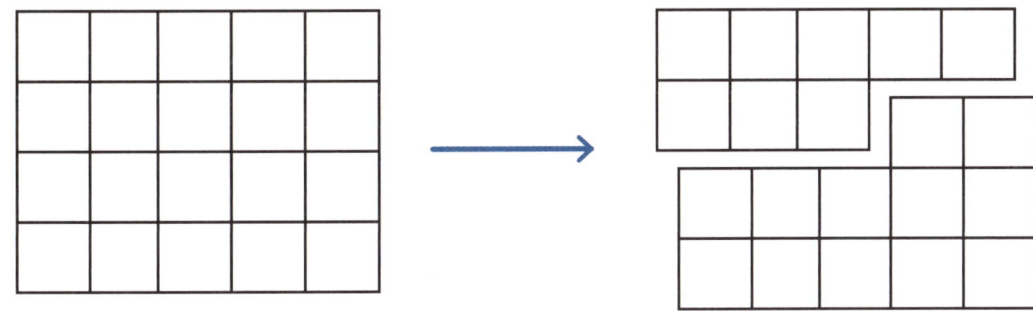

20 made with 8 and 12

Directions: Count the objects in each section. Mark an X on the objects taken away. Color the objects that are left over. Write the amount in each box. Then, use two different colors to show how you decomposed the number.

Subtract & Decompose Numbers to 20

Name: _____

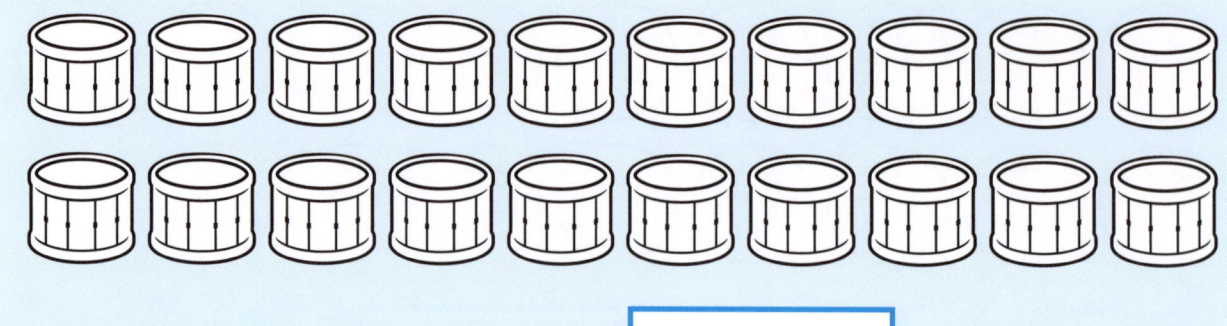

20 − 9 =

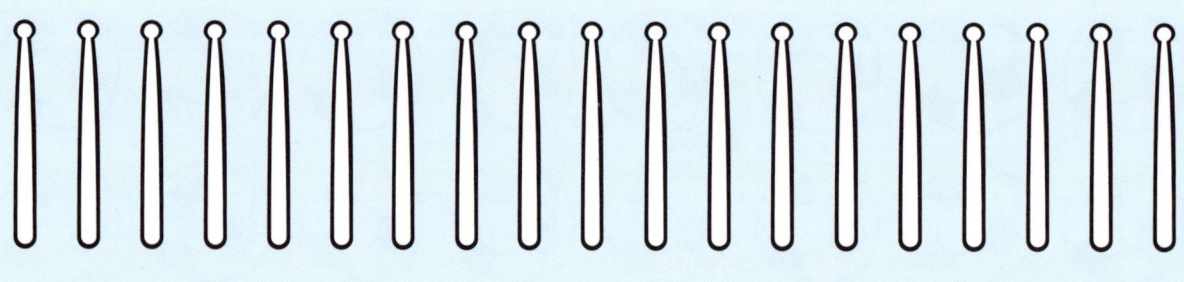

19 − 11 =

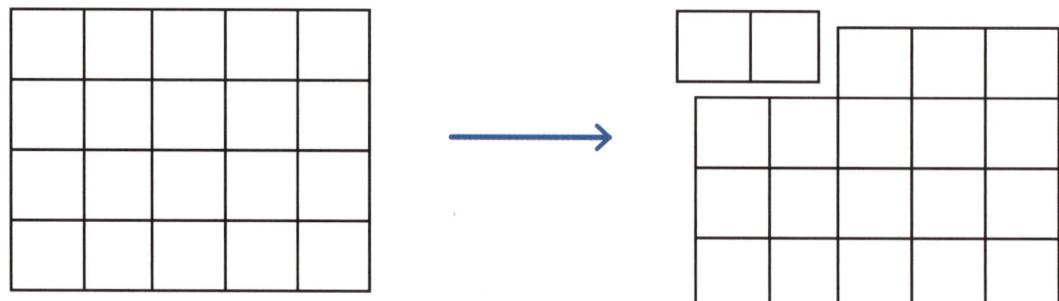

20 made with 2 and 18

Directions: Count the objects in each section. Mark an *X* on the objects taken away. Color the objects that are left over. Write the amount in each box. Then, use two different colors to show how you decomposed the number.

Name: _____

DAY 154

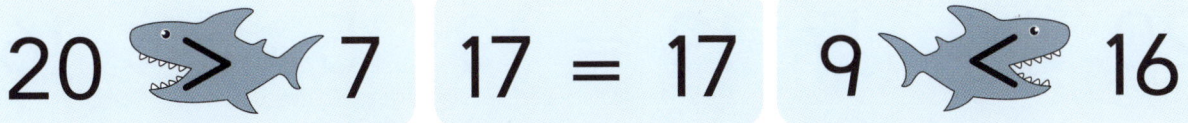

Remember that a shark ALWAYS wants to eat the bigger number!

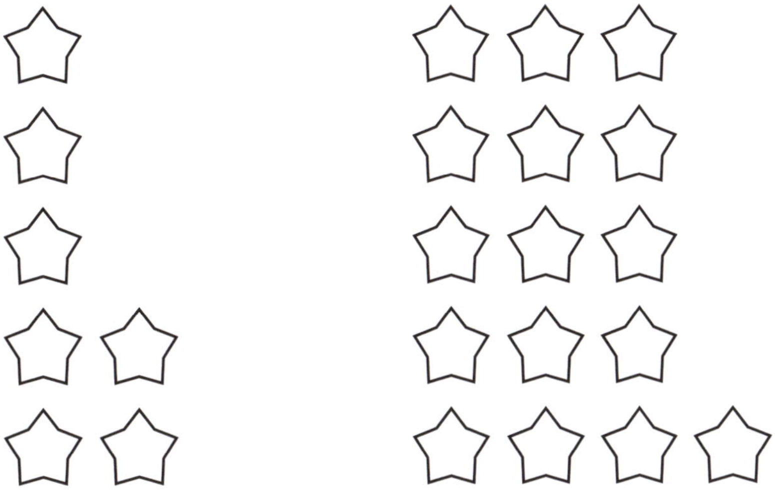

7   > = <   16

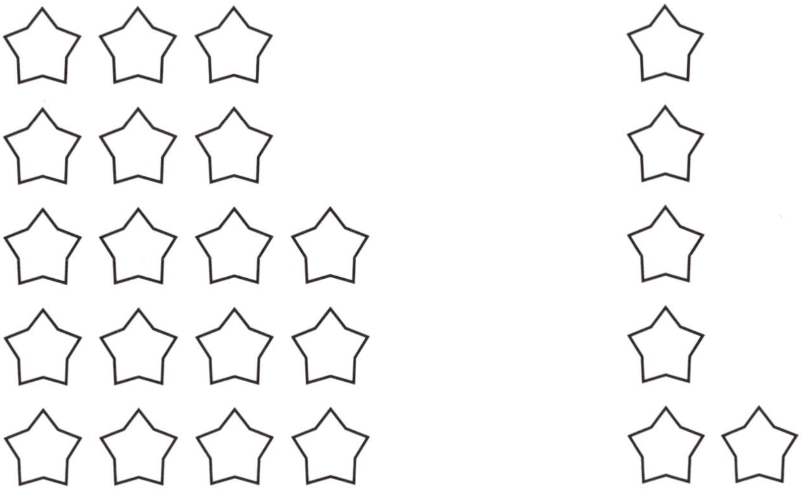

18   > = <   6

Compare Numbers Up to 20

Directions: Count the objects in each section. Compare the two numbers in each section. Circle one of these signs > = <. Color the pictures.

DAY 155

Name: _____

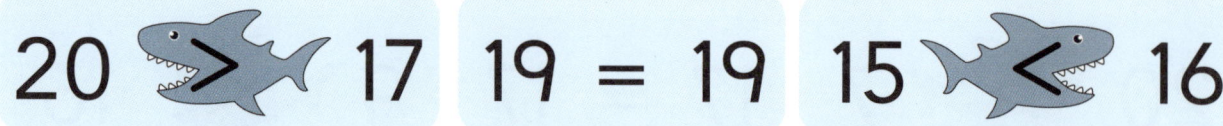

Remember that a shark ALWAYS wants to eat the bigger number!

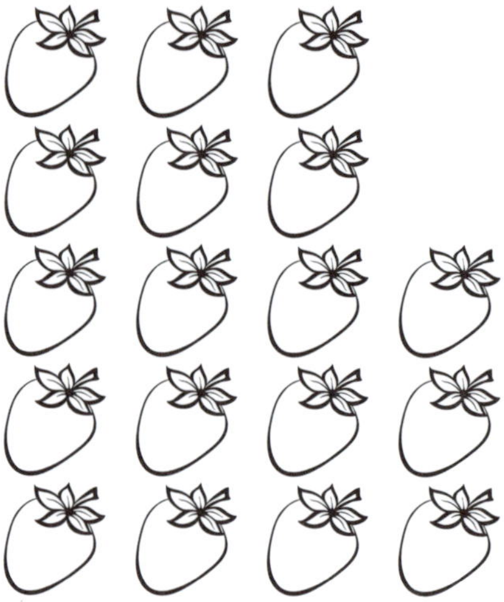

Compare Numbers Up to 20

9   >   =   <   18

20   >   =   <   20

Directions: Count the objects in each section. Compare the two numbers in each section. Circle one of these signs > = <. Color the pictures.

Name: _____

DAY 156

17 > 12   16 = 16   15 < 18

Remember that a shark ALWAYS wants to eat the bigger number!

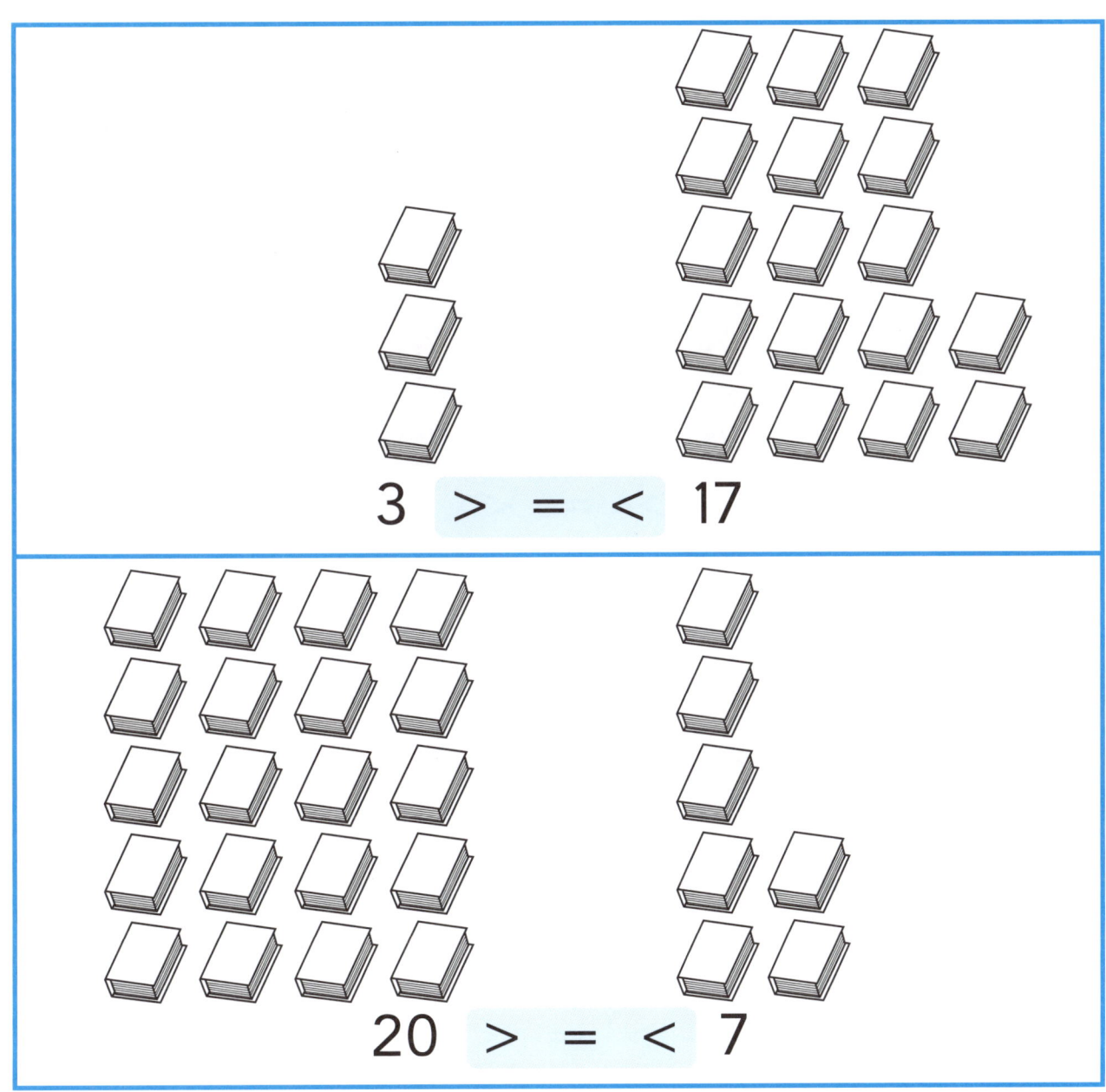

3 > = < 17

20 > = < 7

Compare Numbers Up to 20

Directions: Count the objects in each section. Compare the two numbers in each section. Circle one of these signs > = <. Color the pictures.

DAY 157

Name: _____

18 > 16   20 = 20   15 < 19

Remember that a shark ALWAYS wants to eat the bigger number!

Compare Numbers Up to 20

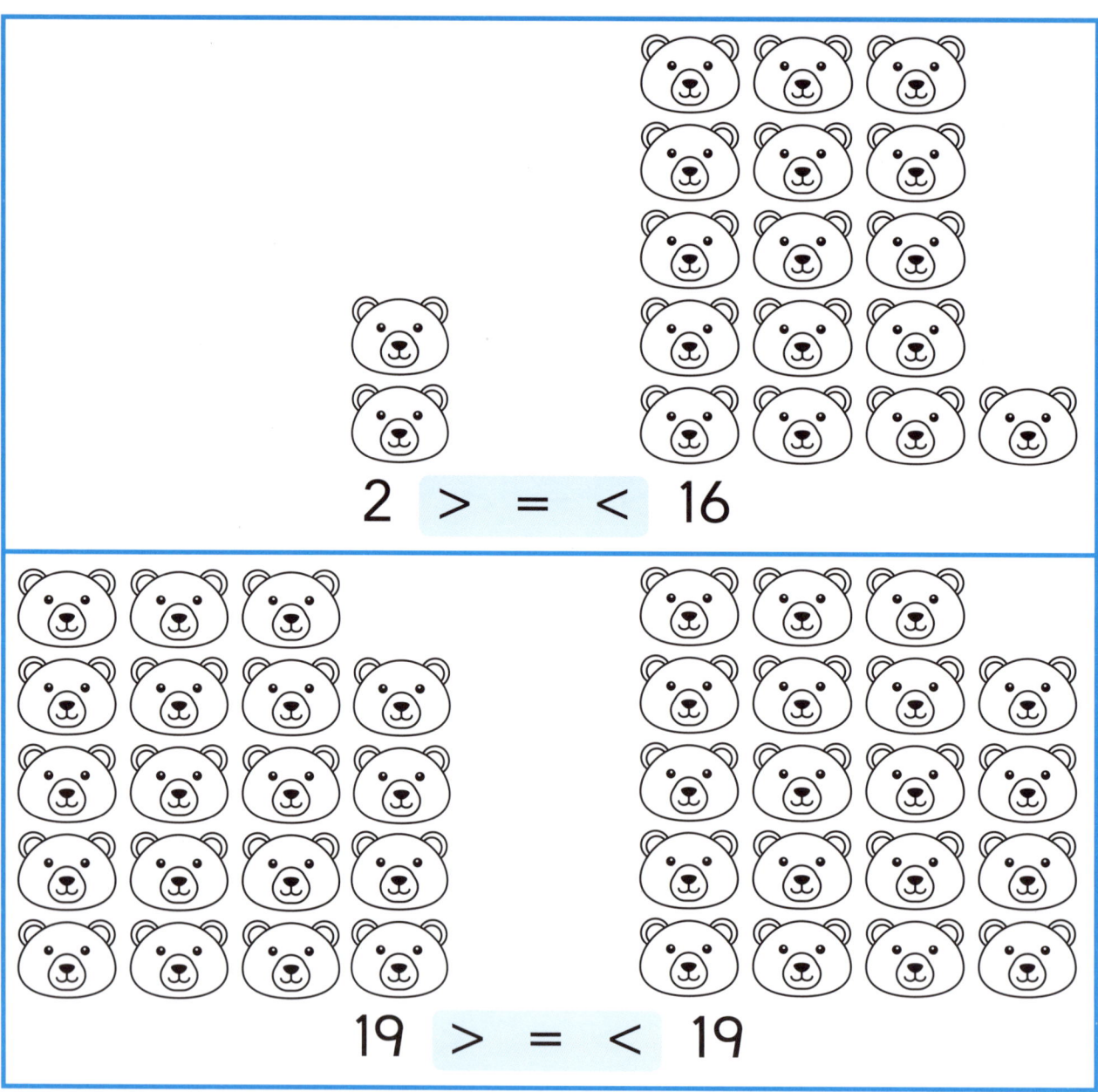

2   > = <   16

19   > = <   19

Directions: Count the objects in each section. Compare the two numbers in each section. Circle one of these signs > = <. Color the pictures.

Name: _____

DAY 158

19 > 18   15 = 15   16 < 18

Remember that a shark ALWAYS wants to eat the bigger number!

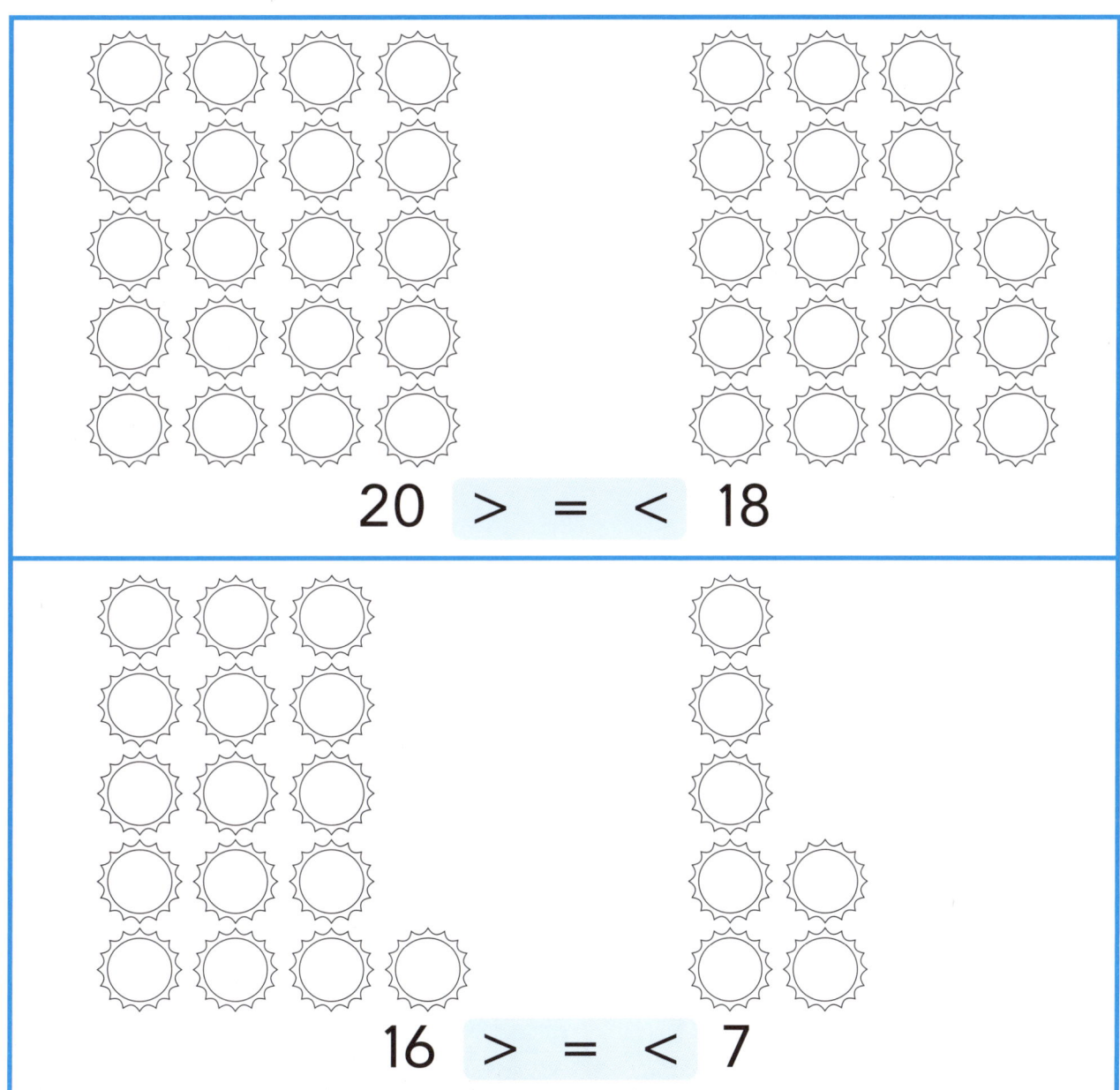

20   > = <   18

16   > = <   7

Compare Numbers Up to 20

Directions: Count the objects in each section. Compare the two numbers in each section. Circle one of these signs > = <. Color the pictures.

Introducing the Concept

Geometry

Learning All About Shapes!

In this section, students learn to identify and name shapes including squares, circles, triangles, rectangles, and hexagons. They learn to describe objects in the environment using names of shapes. Students also describe the relative positions of objects using terms such as *above*, *below*, *beside*, *in front of*, *behind*, and *next to*. Finally, they begin to analyze, compare, create, and compose shapes.

What You May Need

- jumbo pencils or short golf pencils
- crayons, colored pencils, etc.
- small, nonchoking objects for covering-shape activities (modeling clay, interlocking cubes, beans, coins, etc.)

Understanding the Activities

As you work through these pages, here are some ways to further support student learning:

- Discuss the names of the shapes as they are introduced.
- Read the directions to students. Follow the directions one step at a time, allowing enough time for students to complete each task before moving to the next step in the directions.

Name: _____

DAY 159

square

Time to Draw

Directions: Outline all four sides of each square. Color each empty square to match its outline color. Make a square using small objects or clay on the outline of the orange square. Then, draw squares you can see in your community.

Introducing Shapes

Day 160

Name: _____

Introducing Shapes

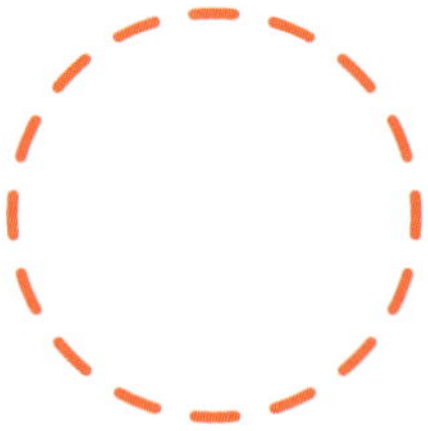

circle

Time to Draw

Directions: Outline each circle. Color each empty circle to match its outline color. Make a circle using small objects or clay on the outline of the purple circle. Then, draw circles you can see in your home.

Name: _____

DAY 161

triangle

Time to Draw

Directions: Outline all three sides of each triangle. Color each empty triangle to match its outline color. Make a triangle using small objects or clay on the outline of the green triangle. Then, draw triangles you can see in your neighborhood.

Introducing Shapes

DAY 162

Name: _____

Introducing Shapes

rectangle

Time to Draw

Directions: Outline all four sides of each rectangle. Color each empty rectangle to match its outline color. Make a rectangle using small objects or clay on the outline of the pink rectangle. Then, draw rectangles you can see in your neighborhood.

Name: _____

DAY 163

hexagon

Directions: Outline all six sides of each hexagon. Color each empty hexagon to match its outline color. Make a hexagon using small objects or clay on the outline of the yellow hexagon. Then, draw hexagons you can see in your home.

Time to Draw

Introducing Shapes

DAY 164

Name: _____

above → 　　　← below

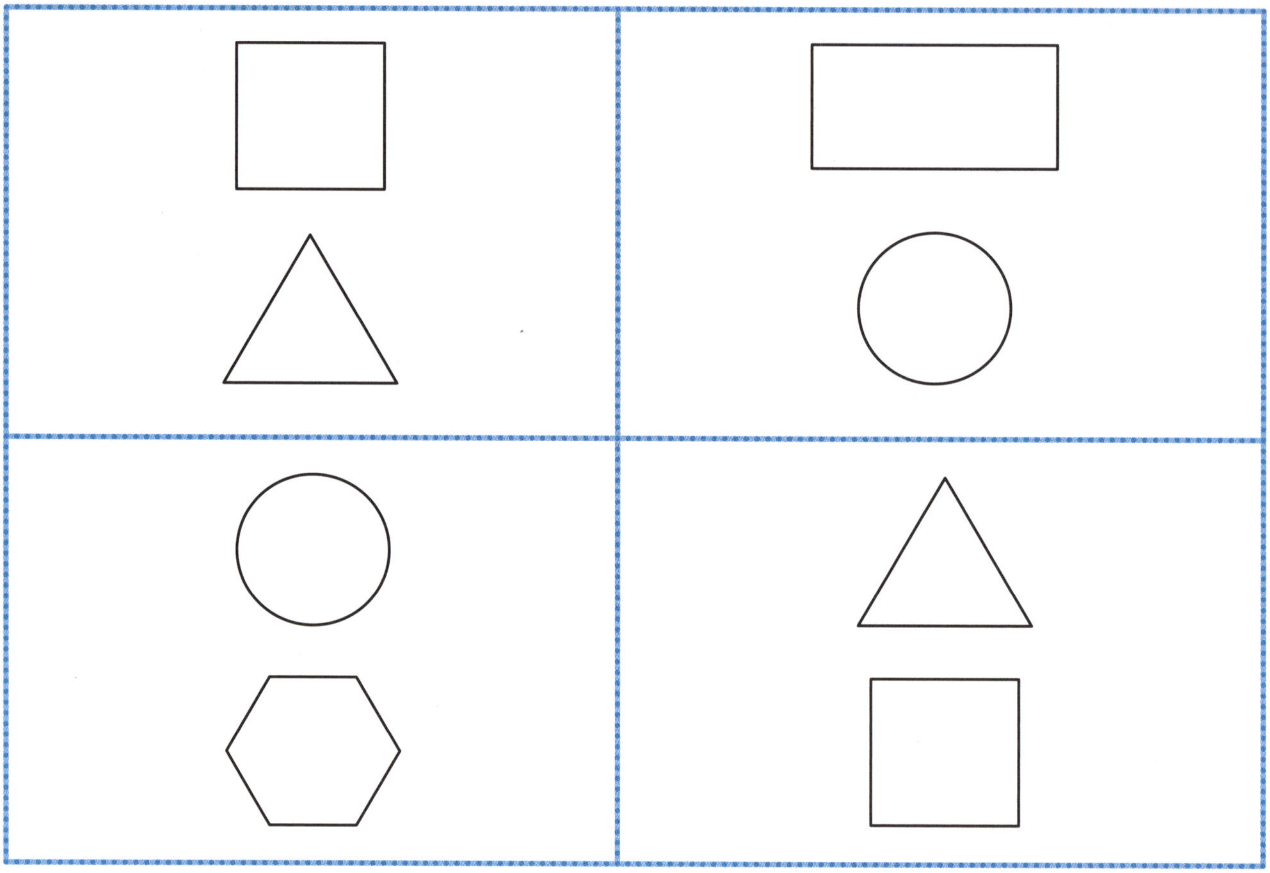

Above & Below

Time to Draw

Directions: In each space, color the shape that is above in blue. Color the shape that is below in red. Then, draw an object you can see that is below another object.

Name: _____

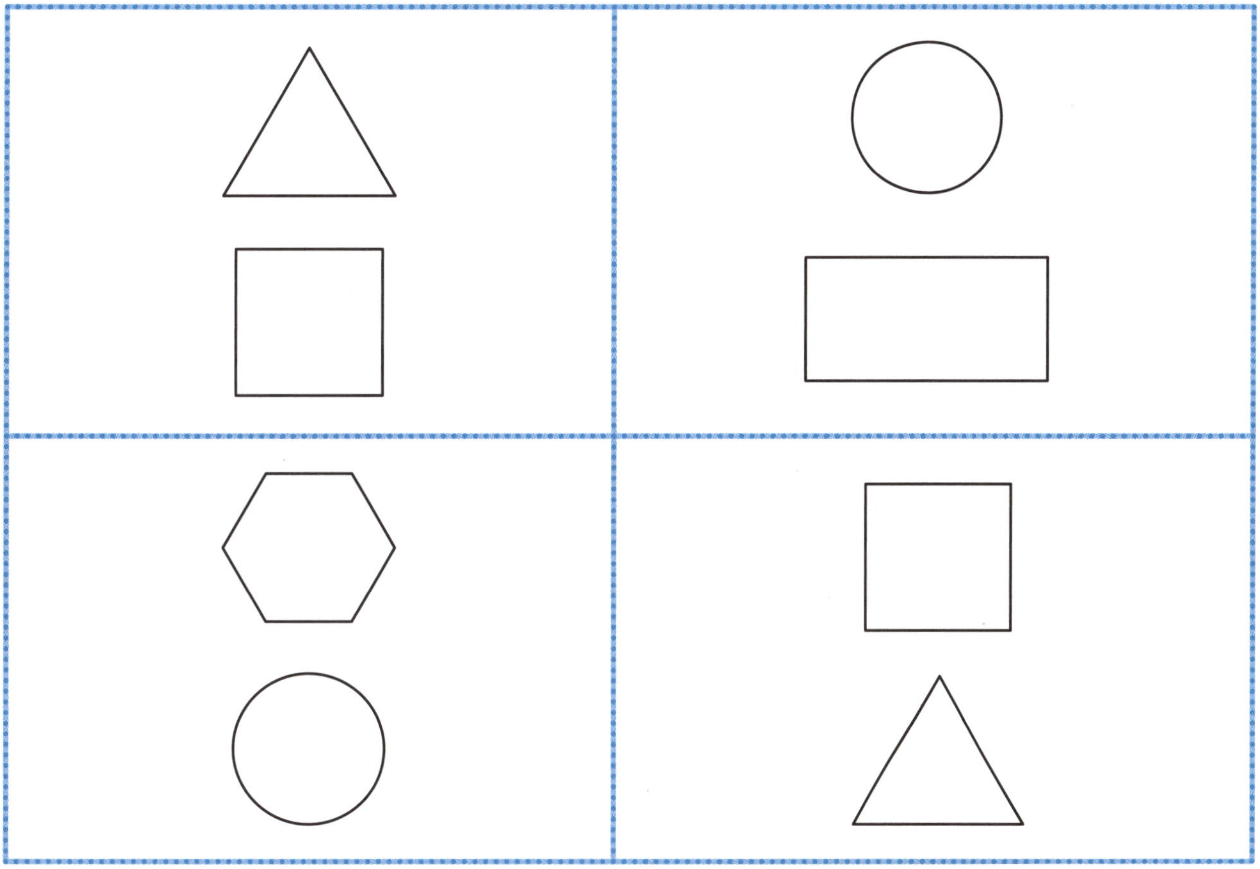

DAY 165

above → below

Above & Below

Time to Draw

Directions: In each space, color the shape that is above in green. Color the shape that is below in yellow. Then, draw an object you can see that is above another object.

DAY 166

Name: _____

above →
← below

Above & Below

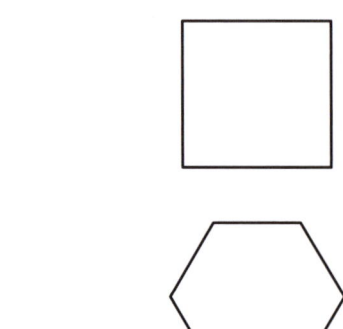 

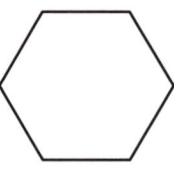 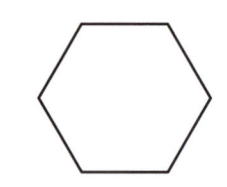

 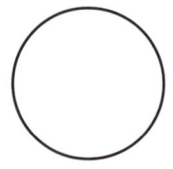

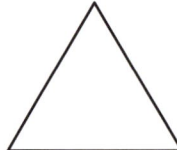 

Time to Draw

Directions: In each space, color the shape that is above in orange. Color the shape that is below in purple. Then, draw an object you can see that is below another object.

Name: _____

DAY 167

Beside & Next To

Time to Draw

Directions: Draw circles next to the lion and the elephant. Draw squares beside the zebra and the hippo. Draw triangles next to the cheetah and the tiger. Color the animals. Then, draw an object you can see that is beside another object.

DAY 168

Name: _____

Beside & Next To

Time to Draw

Directions: Draw circles next to the dolphin and the whale. Draw squares beside the octopus and the sea turtle. Draw triangles next to the fish and the jellyfish. Color the animals. Then, draw an object you can see that is next to another object.

Name: _____

Time to Draw

Directions: Draw circles next to the cow and the horse. Draw squares beside the sheep and the goat. Draw triangles next to the chicken and the donkey. Color the animals. Then, draw an object you can see that is beside another object.

DAY 170

Name: _____

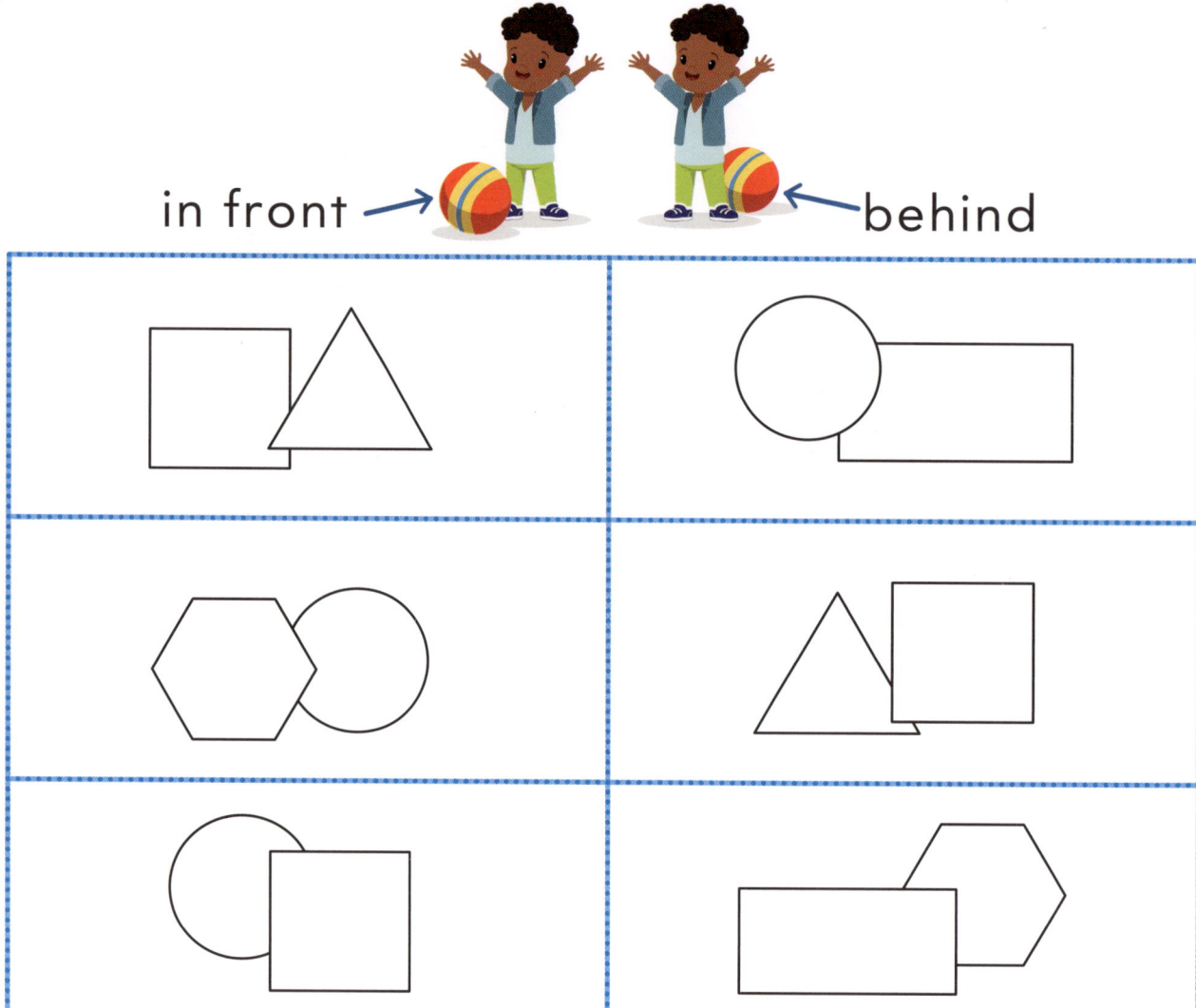

in front / behind

Time to Draw

Directions: In each space, color the shape that is behind in blue. Color the shape that is in front in red. Then, draw an object you can see that is behind another object.

Name: _____

DAY 171

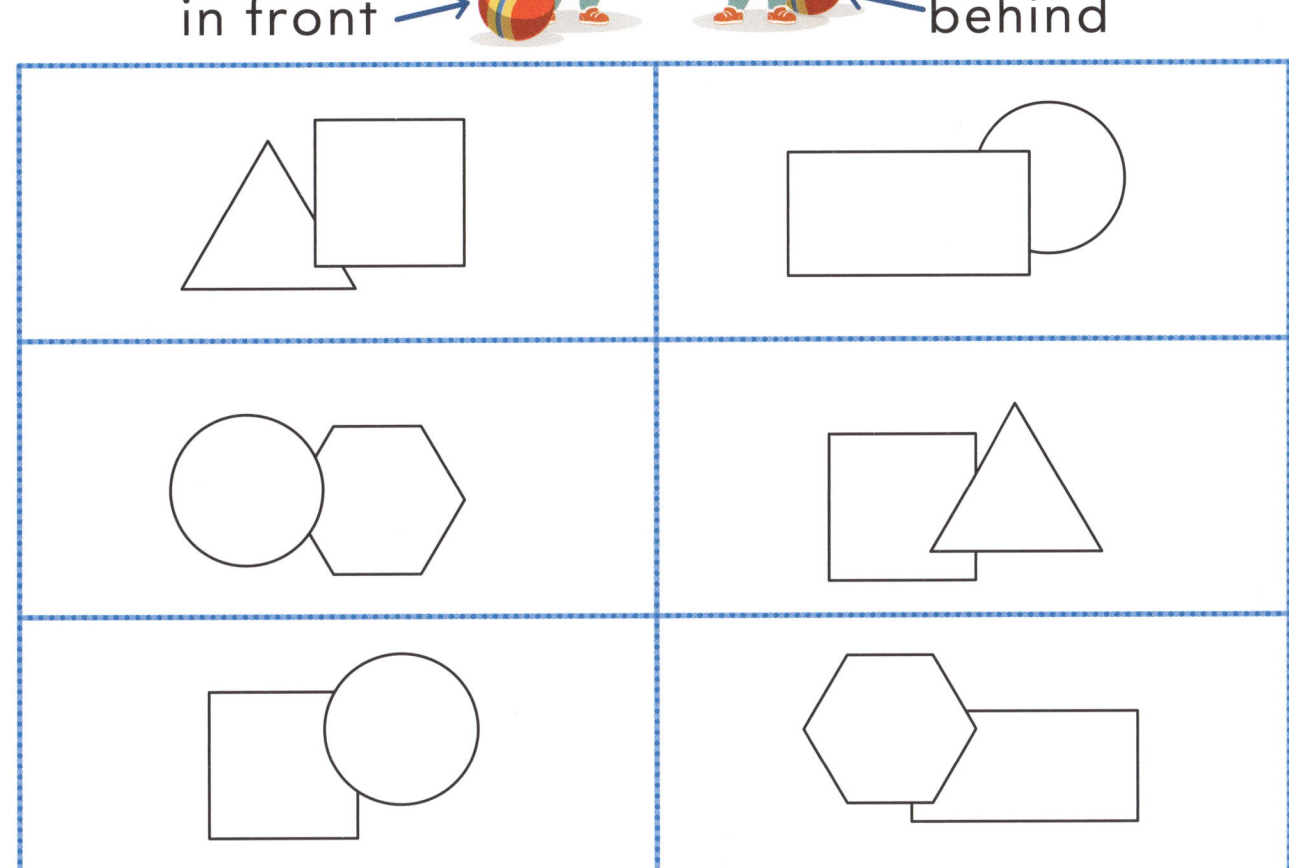

Time to Draw

Directions: In each space, color the shape that is behind in green. Color the shape that is in front in yellow. Then, draw an object you can see that is in front of another object.

Behind & In Front

DAY 172

Name: _____

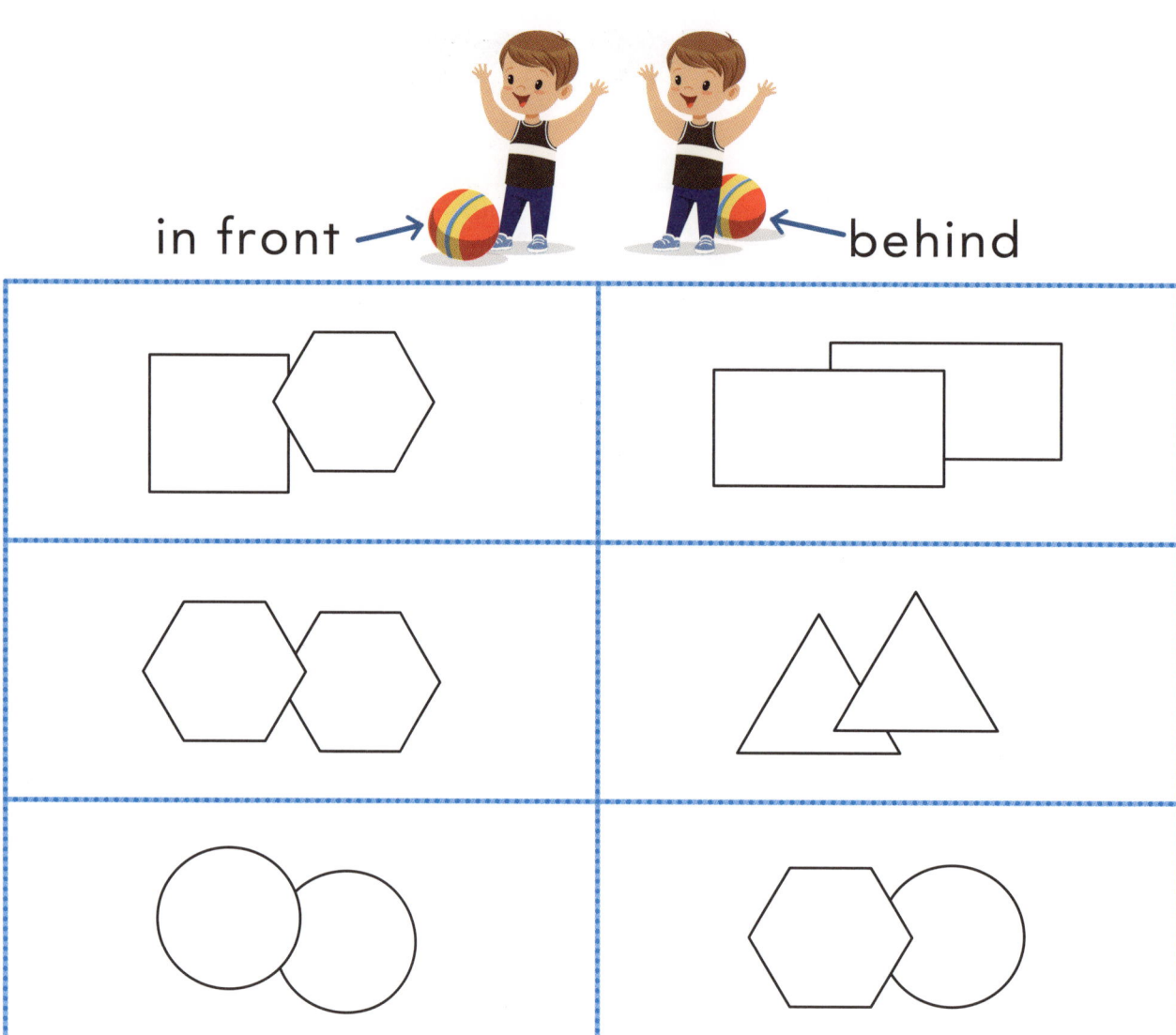

Time to Draw

Directions: In each space, color the shape that is behind in orange. Color the shape that is in front in purple. Then, draw your favorite animal behind your favorite shape.

Name: _____

□	○	△	▭	⬡
orange	purple	green	pink	yellow

Time to Draw

Directions: Use the key to color all the shapes. Put an X on the largest square. Then, draw a small triangle and a large triangle.

DAY 174

Name: _____

Time to Draw

Directions: Use the key to color the hidden shapes. Put an X on the smallest circle. Then, draw a small square and a large square.

Name: _____

□	○	△	▭	⬡
orange	purple	green	pink	yellow

DAY 175

Compare, Create & Compose Shapes

Time to Draw

Directions: Use the key to color the hidden shapes. Put an X on the largest triangle. Then, draw a small circle and a large circle.

DAY 176

Name: _____

10 and 9 make 19 | 20 made with 12 and 8

Directions: Count the socks and goats. Write how many in all. Use two different colors to represent each number to make 19. Decompose the number 20 by using a different color to represent each number. Then, color the pictures.

Name: _____

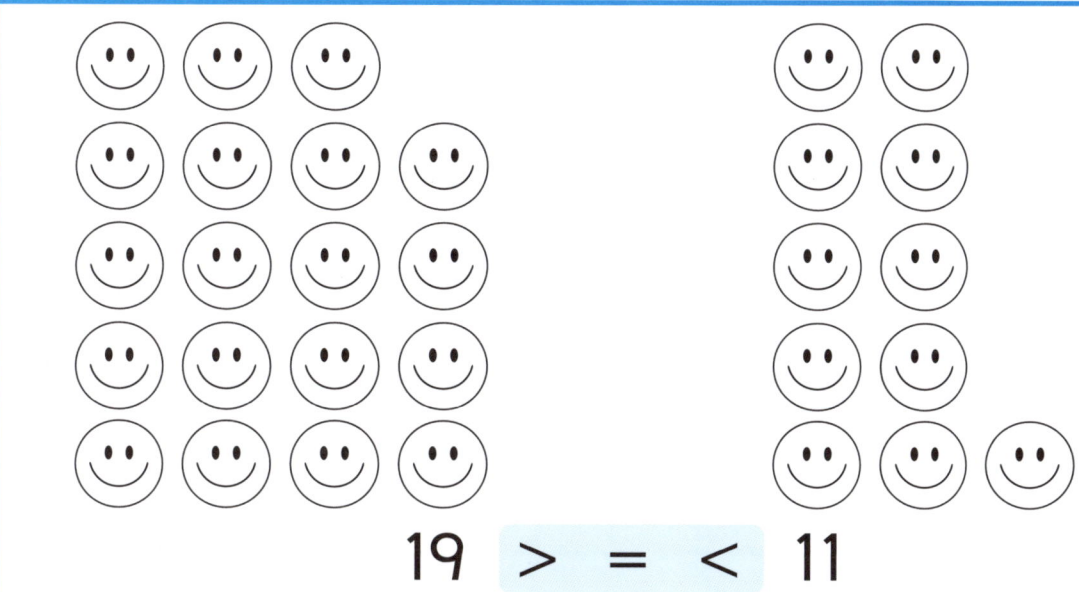

19 > = < 11

Heavy Object	Light Object	Tall Object	Short Object

Directions: Count the faces, and compare the numbers. Circle one of these signs > = <. Circle the animal that is lighter than a glue bottle. Color the pictures. Then, draw heavy, light, tall, and short objects.

Name: _____

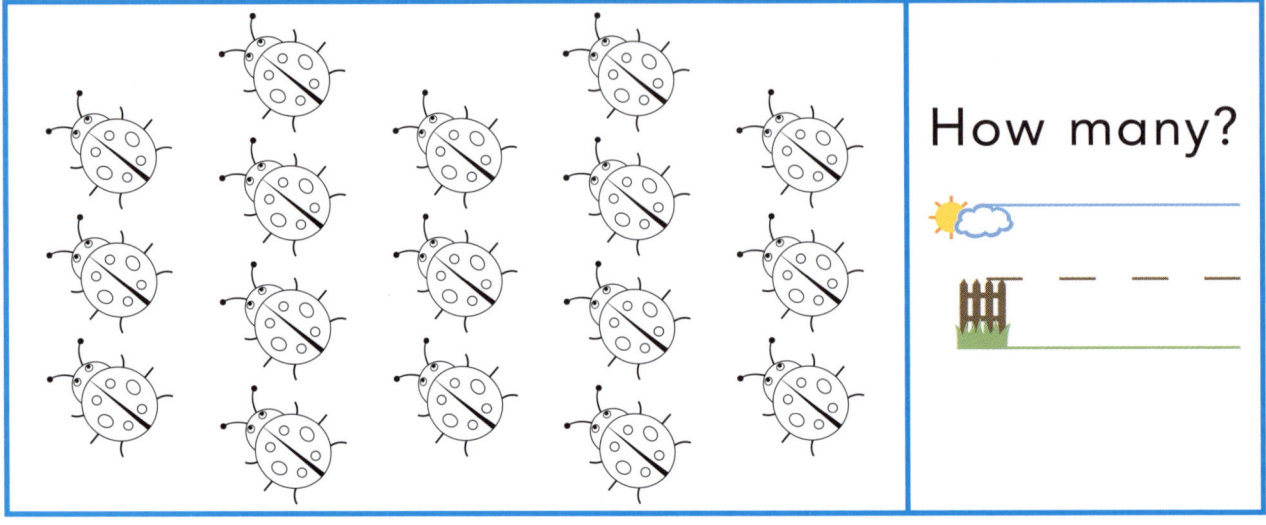

How many?

20	19	20	20	18
18	20	16	17	20
16	17	19	20	17

Count on...

1		3	4	
6	7	8		
11	12		14	15
16		18		20

Directions: Count the ladybugs. Write the number of ladybugs. Color the pictures. Find every number 20, and color those squares in green. Then, count on by ones to fill in the missing numbers.

Name: _____

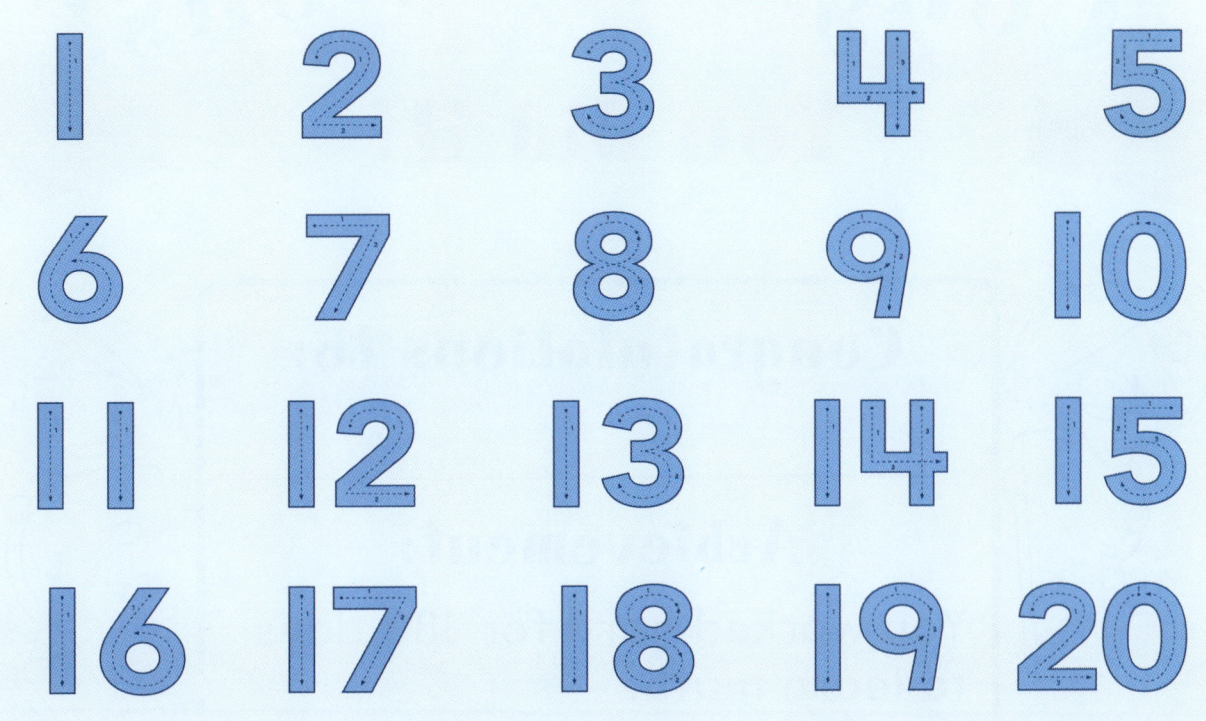

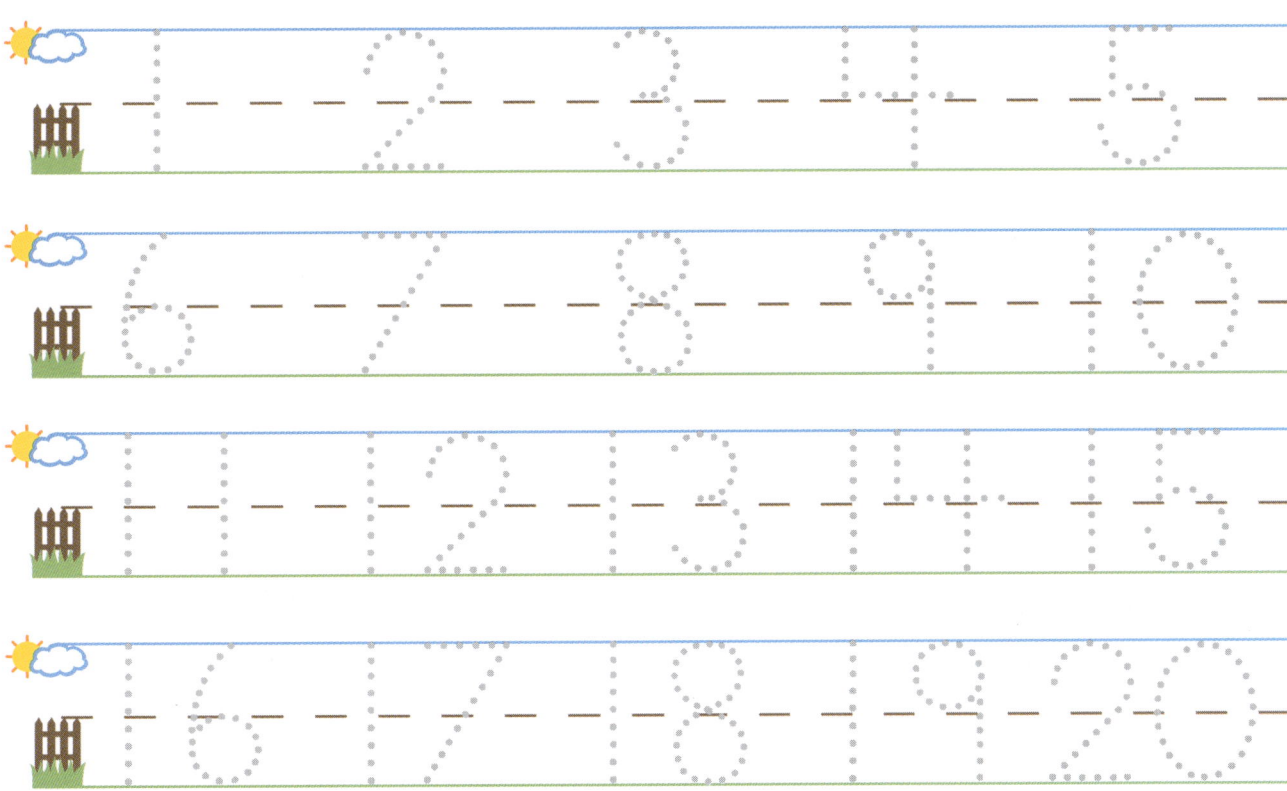

Directions: Touch and say each number. Then, write each number.

DAY 180

Review 0–20, Measurement & Shapes

Congratulations!
You did it!

Congratulations to:
_____

Achievement:
You worked hard for 180 days to learn math!

Way to go! You did your best!

Awarded by: _____ **Date:** _____

Directions: Read each word aloud with an adult. Draw yourself as a mathematician. Post this certificate somewhere special.

Answer Key

page 27

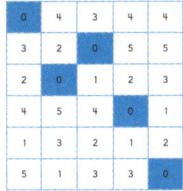

Students should write 5 on the line.

page 29

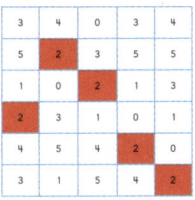

Students should write 5 on the line.

page 31

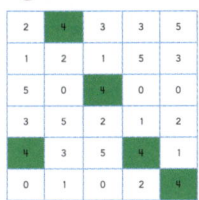

Students should write 5 on the line.

page 38
4 penguins; 3 baseballs; 5 pizza slices

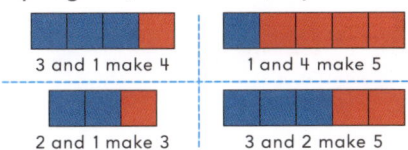

page 39
4 seashells; 3 bags of popcorn; 5 trees

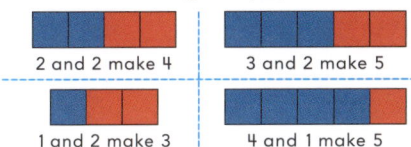

page 40
5 ladybugs; 4 flowers; 3 hamburgers; 2 panda bears

page 41
2 rainbows; 3 dolphins; 4 books; 5 bunnies

page 42
5 monkeys; 4 tennis rackets; 3 lemons

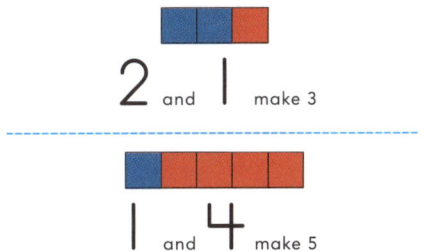

page 43
2 whales; 1 skateboard

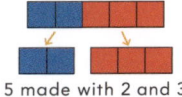

5 made with 2 and 3

page 44
0 grasshoppers; 1 watermelon slice

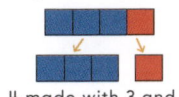

4 made with 3 and 1

page 45
1 lizard; 0 bananas

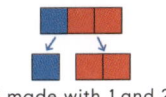

3 made with 1 and 2

page 46
2 suns; 1 strawberry

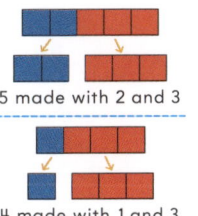

5 made with 2 and 3

4 made with 1 and 3

page 47
1 moon; 3 whales; 2 oranges; 2 pencils

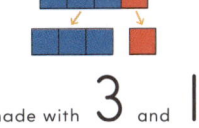

4 made with 3 and 1

page 48
3 > 2; 4 > 1; 1 < 2

page 49
5 = 5; 4 > 2; 3 > 1; 3 < 5

page 50
4 > 3; 3 = 3; 2 < 5; 5 > 4

Answer Key (cont.)

page 51
5 > 2; 3 > 2; 4 > 1; 4 = 4

page 52
4 > 3; 2 = 2; Students should trace the greater than sign.

page 63

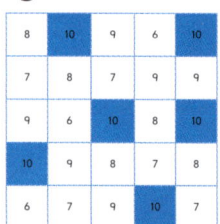

Students should write 4 on the line.

page 65

Students should write 5 on the line.

page 67

Students should write 6 on the line.

page 73
6 dinosaurs; 7 tennis rackets; 9 orange slices; 8 elephants

 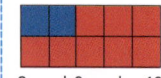
4 and 6 make 10 | 2 and 8 make 10

page 74
8 bunnies; 9 crabs; 7 popsicles; 7 suns

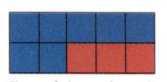 
7 and 3 make 10 | 9 and 1 make 10

page 75
8 caterpillars; 7 sunflowers; 6 hot dogs; 6 gorillas

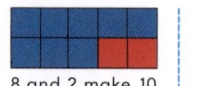 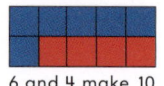
8 and 2 make 10 | 6 and 4 make 10

page 76
8 whales; 7 books; 8 skeletons; 6 horses

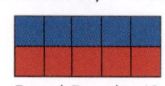 
5 and 5 make 10 | 3 and 7 make 10

page 77
7 hedgehogs; 8 shoes; 6 carrots; 6 watches

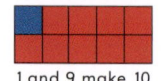 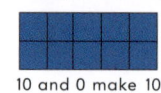
1 and 9 make 10 | 10 and 0 make 10

page 78
7 cowboy hats; 6 mittens

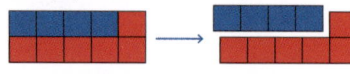
10 made with 4 and 6

page 79
4 circles; 6 pears

10 made with 5 and 5

page 80
2 clouds; 5 bananas

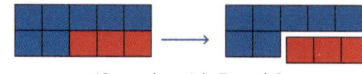
10 made with 7 and 3

page 81
2 suns; 3 turtles

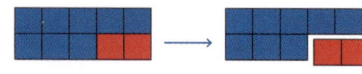
10 made with 8 and 2

page 82
4 moons; 1 orange

10 made with 10 and 0

page 83
9 > 6; 8 = 8; 6 < 7

page 84
5 < 8; 3 > 2; 2 < 9; 4 = 4

page 85
6 < 10; 9 > 8; 10 > 7; 9 = 9

Answer Key (cont.)

page 86
9 > 6; 10 > 4; 8 < 9; 7 = 7

page 87
5 = 5; 4 < 9; 2 < 8; 8 > 7

page 89

page 90
twig: 7 cubes; crayon: 4 cubes; marker: 6 cubes; pencil: 8 cubes; paintbrush: 9 cubes
Students should draw the paintbrush in the Longest Object box and draw the crayon in the Shortest Object box.

page 91

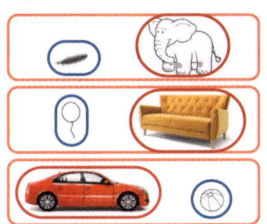

page 92
Students should circle the penny, feather, and key. Students should draw the hippopotamus in the Heaviest Object box and draw the feather in the Lightest Object box.

page 93

page 94
robot: 6 cubes; teddy bear: 5 cubes; doll: 7 cubes; rocket ship: 8 cubes
Students should draw the rocket ship in the Tallest Object box and the teddy bear in the Shortest Object box.

page 95
Students should circle the scooter, bandana, whisk, green beetle, and the dog on the left.

page 96
Students should circle the red candle, the windmill, the skyscraper, and the grandfather clock.

page 97
Students should circle the red ball, the honeybee, the leaf, and the grape.

page 98
Students should circle the chopsticks, the eraser on the left, the glue bottle, the highlighter, and the scissors on the left.

page 99
Students should circle the girl, the lamp on the right, the boy, and the stepstool.

page 100
Students should circle the rabbit, the house, the bed, the tractor, and the football. Students should write 3 on the line.

page 101
Students should circle the screw, the pencil, and the turtle. Students should color 3 Short Objects and 4 Long Objects.

page 102
Students should circle the apple, the toy car, the feather, and the fish. Students should color 4 Light Objects and 4 Heavy Objects.

page 103
Students should circle the shoe, the key, the nail, the baby, and the teddy bear. Students should color 5 Short Objects and 3 Tall Objects.

page 104
Students should circle all the large objects. Check to see that students have counted and colored the correct amount of Large Objects and Small Objects based on their drawings.

page 116

11	15	14	15	13
15	13	15	11	12
13	11	12	14	14
12	14	11	13	15
14	12	14	12	11

Students should write 5 on the line.

Answer Key (cont.)

page 118

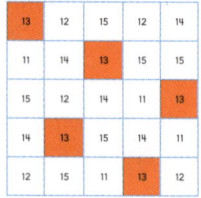

Students should write 5 on the line.

page 120

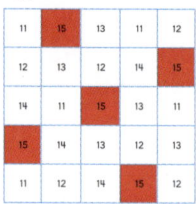

Students should write 5 on the line.

page 126

11 zebras; 13 robots
6 + 6 = 12

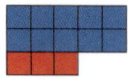

10 and 3 make 13

page 127

14 flamingos; 14 trains
9 + 2 = 11

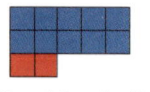 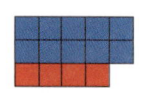

10 and 2 make 12   10 and 4 make 14

page 128

15 smiley faces; 11 jelly beans
5 + 9 = 14

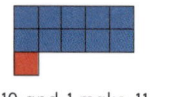 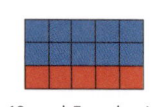

10 and 1 make 11   10 and 5 make 15

page 129

13 balloons; 14 bananas
3 + 8 = 11

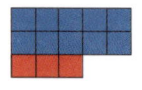 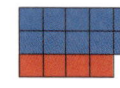

10 and 3 make 13   10 and 4 make 14

page 130

13 paper airplanes; 15 candies
5 + 6 = 11

10 and 5 make 15   10 and 2 make 12

page 131

8 cookies; 3 olives

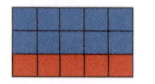 

15 made with 10 and 5

page 132

6 spoons; 9 sunglasses

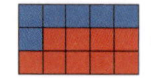 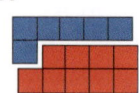

15 made with 6 and 9

page 133

10 pineapples; 4 goldfish

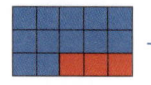 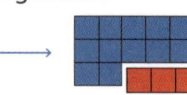

15 made with 12 and 3

page 134

7 kites; 8 plants

 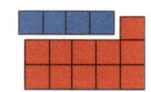

15 made with 4 and 11

page 135

4 bags of popcorn; 10 rocket ships

 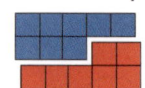

15 made with 8 and 7

page 136

7 < 14; 13 > 6

page 137

15 > 8; 13 > 2

page 138

11 > 8; 13 > 6

page 139

12 > 6; 14 > 7

page 140

15 = 15; 2 < 12

Answer Key (cont.)

page 151

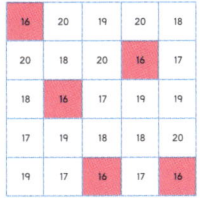

Students should write 5 on the line.

page 153

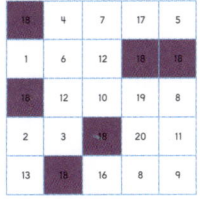

Students should write 6 on the line.

page 155

Students should write 6 on the line.

page 161
16 kiwis (birds); 19 tops

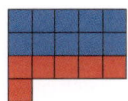

10 and 6 make 16

page 162
17 seals; 20 seahorses

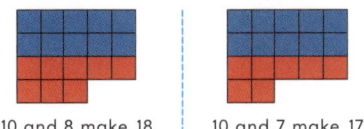

10 and 8 make 18 | 10 and 7 make 17

page 163
18 smiley faces; 16 cucumber slices

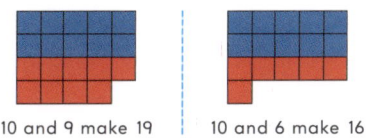

10 and 9 make 19 | 10 and 6 make 16

page 164
19 beach balls; 17 beads

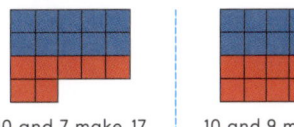

10 and 7 make 17 | 10 and 9 make 19

page 165
17 blue ribbons; 18 gumdrops

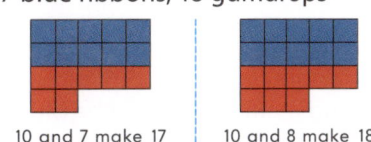

10 and 7 make 17 | 10 and 8 make 18

page 166
9 wheels; 8 keys

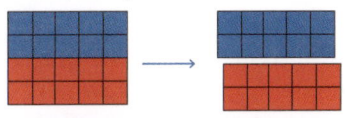

20 made with 10 and 10

page 167
13 buns; 11 slices of cake

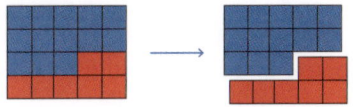

20 made with 13 and 7

page 168
12 lizards; 12 trumpets

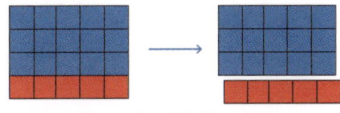

20 made with 15 and 5

page 169
13 coconuts; 5 soccer balls

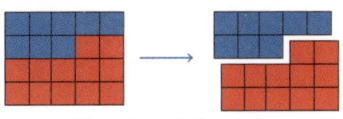

20 made with 8 and 12

page 170
11 drums; 8 drumsticks

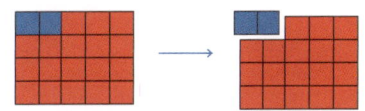

20 made with 2 and 18

page 171
7 < 16; 18 > 6

Answer Key (cont.)

page 172
9 < 18; 20 = 20

page 173
3 < 17; 20 > 7

page 174
2 < 16; 19 = 19

page 175
20 > 18; 16 > 7

page 182
Top row: square and rectangle should be blue; triangle and circle should be red
Bottom row: circle and triangle should be blue; hexagon and square should be red

page 183
Top row: triangle and circle should be green; square and rectangle should be yellow
Bottom row: hexagon and square should be green; circle and triangle should be yellow

page 184
Top row: square and rectangle should be orange; both hexagons should be purple
Bottom row: square and circle should be orange; triangle and square should be purple

page 185

page 186

page 187

page 188
First row: square and rectangle should be blue; triangle and circle should be red
Middle row: circle and triangle should be blue; hexagon and square should be red
Bottom row: circle and hexagon should be blue; square and rectangle should be red

page 189
First row: triangle and circle should be green; square and rectangle should be yellow
Middle row: hexagon and square should be green; circle and triangle should be yellow
Bottom row: square and rectangle should be green; circle and hexagon should be yellow

page 190
First row: square and rectangle on the right should be orange; hexagon and rectangle on the left should be purple
Middle row: hexagon on the right and triangle on the left should be orange; hexagon on the left and triangle on the right should be purple
Bottom row: both circles on the right should be orange; circle on the left and hexagon should be purple

page 191

Answer Key (cont.)

page 192

page 193

page 194

18 socks; 17 goats

10 and 9 make 19 | 20 made with 12 and 8

page 195

19 > 11

Students should circle the ant. Check that students have drawn heavy, light, tall, and short objects in the correct boxes.

page 196

17 ladybugs

20	19	20	20	18
18	20	16	17	20
16	17	19	20	17

1	**2**	3	4	**5**
6	7	8	**9**	**10**
11	12	**13**	14	15
16	**17**	18	**19**	20

Appendix

References Cited

California Department of Education. 2012. *The Alignment of the California Preschool Learning Foundations with Key Early Education Resources.* Sacramento: California Department of Education.

Duncan, Greg J., Chantelle J. Dowsett, Amy Claessens, Katherine Magnuson, Aletha C. Huston, Pamela Klebanov, Linda S. Pagani, Leon Feinstein, Mimi Engel, Jeanne Brooks-Gunn, Holly Sexton, Kathryn Duckworth, and Crista Japel. 2007. "School Readiness and Later Achievement." *Developmental Psychology* 43 (6): 1428–1446.

First Things First. 2017. "Early Childhood Brain Development Has Lifelong Impact." *Arizona PBS*. azpbs.org/2017/11/early-childhood-brain-development-lifelong-impact.

Hirsch, Megan. 2010. *How To Hold a Pencil.* Los Angeles: Hirsch Indie Press.

Marzano, Robert. 2010. "Art and Science of Teaching: When Practice Makes Perfect…Sense." *Educational Leadership* 68 (3): 81–83. www.ascd.org/publications/educational-leadership/nov10/vol68/num03/When-Practice-Makes-Perfect-%E2%80%A6-Sense.aspx.

McCray, Jennifer S., Jie-Qi Chen, and Janet Eisenband Sorkin, eds. 2019. *Growing Mathematical Minds: Conversations Between Developmental Psychologists and Early Childhood Teachers.* New York: Routledge.

Suggested Websites

Website Title	Address	Content
ABC Mouse	abcmouse.com	This site includes varied math content. Short videos can also be found on YouTube (free or subscription to access all content).
Didax	didax.com/math/virtual-manipulatives.html	Use virtual math manipulatives to practice counting and cardinality skills.
eSpark Learning	esparklearning.com	Complete differentiated math activities.
MathRack	mathrack.com	Purchase hands-on tools for a class and/or students to use to count. You can use a MathRack of 5, 10, or 20.
Starfall	www.starfall.com	This site includes varied math content.

Appendix

Digital Resources

Accessing the Digital Resources

The digital resources can be downloaded by following these steps:

1. Go to www.tcmpub.com/digital

2. Use the ISBN number to redeem the digital resources.

3. Respond to the question using the book.

4. Follow the prompts on the Content Cloud website to sign in or create a new account.

5. The content redeemed will now be on your My Content screen. Click on the product to look through the digital resources. All resources are available for download. Select files can be previewed, opened, and shared. For questions and assistance with your license key card, or to report a lost card, please contact Shell Education.

mail: customerservice@tcmpub.com
phone: 800-858-7339

ISBN:

 **CONTENTS OF THE DIGITAL RESOURCES**

Teacher Resources
- Introducing the Concept pages
- Certificate of Completion
- Standards Correlation

Activities
- Ideas for extending the learning to real-world situations
- Templates for creating word pattern books
- Hands-on practice for learning uppercase and lowercase letters
- Writing practice of uppercase and lowercase letters

Doodles